Introducing
psychology through
research

Introducing psychology through research

Amanda Albon

Open University Press

Open University Press
McGraw-Hill Education
McGraw-Hill House
Shoppenhangers Road
Maidenhead
Berkshire
England
SL6 2QL

email: enquiries@openup.co.uk
world wide web: www.openup.co.uk

and Two Penn Plaza, New York, NY 10121-2289, USA

First published 2007

A catalogue record of this book is available from the British Library

ISBN-10: 0335 221 343 (pb) 0335 221 351 (hb)
ISBN-13: 978 0335 221 349 (pb) 978 0335 221 356 (hb)

Library of Congress Cataloging-in-Publication Data
CIP data applied for

Typeset by RefineCatch Limited, Bungay, Suffolk
Printed in Poland by OZ Graf. S.A.
www.polskabook.pl

The *McGraw·Hill Companies*

For Nick, Saskia and Hugo Tatt; my loved ones.

Contents

List of boxes and tables

Boxes

Tables

Acknowledgements

Foremost, I would like to thank Open University Press, especially Laura Dent, Shona Mullen and Ruben Hale for their help and advice. Thanks also to Nick for reading many drafts, to the anonymous reviewers who provided helpful comments and criticisms, and to Elizabeth Haylett at the Society of Authors.

Thanks are also due to two groups of students who inspired me to write this book. I taught the first group for a University of Kent programme at Canterbury Adult Education Centre from 2004 to 2005. They had no previous knowledge of psychology and many initially held misconceptions about what psychology was. To their credit, they stuck with my course! The second were a group studying with the Open University. They reminded me that the leap from using text books to using journal research papers can be very daunting.

Copyright acknowledgements

I am grateful for permission to reprint the following material:

Chapter 3: Searching for threat, *The Quarterly Journal of Experimental Psychology*, (2002), by kind permission of the Experimental Psychology Society, 2006.

Chapter 4: Reprinted from the *Journal of Verbal Learning and Verbal Behaviour*, 13, Loftus, E.F. and Palmer, J.C., Reconstruction of automobile destruction: an example of the interaction between language and memory, 585–9, (1974), with permission from Elsevier.

Chapter 5: *European Journal of Social Psychology*, Fischer, P., Greitemeyer, T., Pollozek, F. and Frey, D. (2006). The unresponsive bystander: are bystanders more responsive in dangerous emergencies?, reproduced by permission of John Wiley and Sons Limited.

Chapter 6: Bokhorst, C.L., Bakermans-Kranenburg, M.J., Fearon, R.M.P., Van Ijzendoorn, M.H., Fonagy, P. and Schuengel, C. (2003). The importance of shared environment in mother-infant attachment security: a behavioural genetic study. *Child Development*, 74: 1769–82, by kind permission of Blackwell Publishing.

Chapter 7: Reprinted from *Intelligence*, 33, McDaniel, M. Big-brained people are smarter: a meta-analysis of the relationship between in vivo brain volume and intelligence, 337–46, (2005), with permission from Elsevier.

Chapter 8: Costa, P.T. and McCrae, R.R. (1988). Personality in adulthood: a six-year longitudinal study of self-reports and spouse ratings on the NEO Personality Inventory, *Journal of Personality and Social Psychology*, 54 (5), 853–63, in the public domain.

Chapter 9: Startup, M., Jackson, M.C., Evans, K.E. and Bendix, S. North Wales randomized controlled trial of cognitive behaviour therapy for acute schizophrenia spectrum disorders: two-year follow-up and economic evaluation, *Psychological Medicine*, (2005), © Cambridge University Press, reproduced with permission.

Chapter 10: Milgram, S. (1963). Behavioral Study of Obedience, *Journal of Abnormal and Social Psychology*, 67(4), 371–8, permission granted by Alexandra Milgram.

Introduction

Why have you picked up this book? Maybe you are curious about what psychology involves. Maybe you are already studying psychology and are looking for more information. No, this is not an interrogation! It is exactly this type of curiosity about people's actions that makes psychology what it is – a wide-ranging and fascinating subject which gives us insight into human behaviour.

I first picked up a book on psychology, in a local library, at the age of 20 with very little idea of what psychology actually was. By the time I had read a couple of chapters I was absolutely hooked. I had learnt many facts, such as why people can be prejudiced, what attracts one person to another and that we have different types of memory. It also exploded quite a few myths about what psychology was. I was drawn in and driven to find out more. I started a psychology degree as a mature student with little idea of what I was to encounter, but in no way was I disappointed.

Who is this book for?

This book is for anyone who is curious about their own and other people's behaviour. You may be studying psychology at school or university, attending an adult education course, or just interested in what makes us tick. It is intended for you all. You do not need any previous psychology knowledge to understand or enjoy this book. If you are already studying psychology, this book will also help you to look at research papers in journals for the first time. I hope to show you that journal papers are not as inaccessible and frightening as they may first appear!

For whichever reason you chose this book, I hope that you find it informative and stimulating. My goal is to introduce you to psychology by looking at what psychology is, how it is done and reviewing a selection of the topics it covers. It gives a 'taster' of what psychology is as a whole. Chapters 1, 2 and 3 describe what psychology is, the research methods used and how psychologists report their findings. Chapters 4 to 9, each dip into one area of psychology by examining what that area involves and looking at one experiment in depth, using the original research paper. Chapter 10 focuses on the ethics of doing psychological research. The book concludes in chapter 11 by reviewing its contents and providing more information about how to continue learning about psychology and careers in psychology.

How to read this book

If you are new to psychology, I recommend that you start from here and read Chapters 1, 2 and 3. Once you have read these, and have a foundation in psychology, you can either carry on to the end of the book or dip into each chapter as it takes your interest. Each chapter can be read as its own unit; new terms (highlighted in bold in the text) are explained in the glossary at the end of the book or by referring you to the explanation elsewhere in the book. If you are studying psychology, you may already know enough about the subject to go straight into the chapters that cover the core topics (starting at Chapter 4). Again, you can either read from beginning to the end or dip into each chapter as it takes your interest. For all readers, Chapter 11 reviews the book and provides advice about how to continue in psychology, by study or as a career.

PART 1
Introducing psychology

This book is divided into three parts. Part 1 contains three chapters. Chapter 1 explains what psychology is, Chapter 2 looks at the methods psychologists use to study our behaviour and Chapter 3 describes how the findings of such studies are reported. If you are new to psychology, I would advise you to read these next three chapters first, as they will help you to understand the rest of the book.

1 Introducing psychology

It is generally known that psychology is about people, but what exactly does psychology involve? What does it study about people and how does it do so? In this chapter, I will introduce you to psychology by examining what it is, and what it is not! We will also look at how it came to be a distinct subject and why it is largely regarded as a science.

What is psychology?

We are all interested in human behaviour. We regularly speculate about our own and other people's acts in our day-to-day lives. For instance, we wonder 'why did she say that?' or 'why do I forget to do things?' Also our sayings, such as 'birds of a feather flock together', reveal how we try to make sense of behaviour by creating rules of thumb. It is a rare person who does not try to work out how and why other people act and react the way they do, and what their thoughts and feelings are based on. Since we are all familiar with human behaviour, it can appear not to be a worthy subject to study. Indeed, if you mention to a friend or relative that you are reading about or studying psychology, you may well get the response 'Isn't it just common sense?' As psychology involves looking at everyday behaviour, it is often viewed as just common sense dressed up as science. But how far does common sense get us in understanding human behaviour? Consider the following statements:

'Our memory is more accurate when we are hypnotized'
'Not everybody dreams every night'
'The more **bystanders** there are at an emergency, the faster the victim will get help'
'We can completely rely on an eyewitness's memory of an event'
'Brainstorming in groups is more effective than working alone'
'We use only ten per cent of our brain'

Are these 'facts' that you already know to be true through common sense? Actually, **evidence** from **research** indicates that these are not true. Clearly, common sense alone cannot take us very far in understanding what factors lay behind our behaviour. Also, returning to our proverbs, we can see that common sense is often contradictory (e.g. 'too many cooks spoil the broth' versus 'many hands make light work'). If common sense is not enough to work out what is correct about our behaviour, then what can we use? This is where the discipline of psychology comes in; it obtains evidence by doing research in order to determine if our ideas about behaviour are actually correct. Before describing what psychology is in more detail, we will review some common ideas about what psychology involves. These ideas may or may not surprise you, but they will all provide more insight into what psychology is (and is not).

What psychology is not

Many people believe that psychology *just* involves hypnosis, therapy or *only* deals with mental illness. Some other common ideas are that psychologists can read your mind, brainwash or analyse you, or will do something devious to you. These are misunderstandings of what psychology is, as a whole subject. We will look at why these are misunderstandings.

Misunderstanding one: psychology is all about analysing you

The misapprehension that psychology is *only* about analysing individuals, appears to stem from the notion that psychology 'equals' Freud (see Box 1.1). Psychology does not solely involve Freud's methods and theories; it encompasses much more. Although some psychology does incorporate his psychoanalytic approach, psychoanalysis is more common in psychotherapy, counselling and psychiatry than in mainstream psychology. An overlap between these disciplines does exist, but the important point here is that psychology is not *only* psychoanalysis (see Box 1.2). Psychology also tends to use different techniques from psychoanalysis. Freud practised his therapy on one individual at a time, which is known as a **case study**. Certain areas of psychology do use case studies, but the majority of psychology involves studying large numbers of people in order to see how people behave in general. While Freud's ideas have had a substantial impact on psychology, not *all* psychology involves analysing people.

Misunderstanding two: psychology involves mind-reading and brainwashing

Mind-reading is where a person can supposedly interpret what another person is thinking or feeling, just by watching or chatting with them. In one sense, we can all read minds; for example, we can judge how another person feels from their expression. However, mind-reading in the sense of knowing what

Box 1.1 Details: Sigmund Freud (1856–1939)

Sigmund Freud was born in Freiberg, Moravia, in 1856 and moved with his family to Vienna in 1860. He was exiled to London in 1938, due to the Nazi invasion of Austria and died in London the following year. Freud was a physician who initially studied **neurology**, but became interested in **hysteria** and how its physical symptoms could appear without obvious physical causes. He suggested that unconscious mental processes influence our behaviour. He established psycho-analysis as a form of therapy. He used **case studies**, providing analysis by using free association and dream analysis. Free association is where the client says whatever comes into their mind, no matter how absurd or obscene, so 'purging' their anxieties (catharsis). Dream analysis is where the analyst deciphers the hidden meanings in the client's report of their dreams.

Freud developed psychoanalytic theory to explain how both personality and disorders develop from childhood. This approach is known as the psychodynamic approach. His approach to understanding everyday mental functioning, and the stages of normal development from infancy to old age, has had a great impact on psychology and psychiatry. The image of Freud's psychoanalytical therapy, with a patient lying on a couch and the analyst sitting close by, is now part of everyday culture. His ideas have been developed further and are still discussed and used today.

another person is actually thinking remains a stunt; it is not part of psychology. Psychologists cannot tell what is on your mind unless you say so! The term brainwashing refers to using coercive techniques to change a person's beliefs or behaviour (this term is not widely used in psychology). Psychologists may research into attitude change or coercion, but it is not true that psychologists will brainwash you.

Misunderstanding three: psychologists do devious experiments

Unfortunately, psychologists can be maligned in the public eye as devious experimenters who use people as 'guinea pigs' for research. Psychologists never set out to harm people, nor would they use a person in their research without their consent. You can be reassured that all psychologists have to adhere to strict **ethical** guidelines. Guidelines are set out by psychological societies, such as the **British Psychological Society** (BPS), the **American Psychological Association** (APA) and the **European Federation of Psychologists' Associations** (EFPA). These guidelines outline how anyone doing psychological research must treat the people (called **participants**) or non-human animals taking part in the research. It is important that participants are confident in the researchers and that there is mutual respect between them.

Box 1.2 Details: the difference between psychiatrists, psychoanalysts and psychologists

- *Psychiatry* is a branch of medicine which diagnoses and treats mental problems, using drug treatments and other methods. Medical doctors can choose to specialize in psychiatry.
- *Psychoanalysis* is a form of psychodynamic therapy. It involves a patient-analyst relationship where the analyst interprets the links between the patient's past experience and current problems. A person training to be a psychoanalyst first goes through analysis themselves, whereas psychiatrists and psychologists are not obliged to go through psychoanalysis in their training.
- *Psychology* differs from both psychoanalysis and psychiatry as it is interested in all people, not just those with psychological problems (although clinical psychologists do help people with mental illnesses). Most psychologists train by first taking a degree in psychology and then specializing by further training in research or in one type of psychology (e.g. educational psychology). Psychologists can choose to go on to train in psychotherapy or counselling psychology, if they so wish (see Chapter 11 for more information).

Table 1.1 summarizes these guidelines (we look at ethics in more detail in Chapter 10).

You may notice that the guidelines mention deception. Deception is used only to ensure that the participants do not know what the aim of the research is. It is sometimes necessary as, if the participants knew the real reason for the investigation, they may change their behaviour to fit (or not fit) into the researcher's aims and expectations. This would mean that their 'true' behaviour was not being measured. For example, Fischer *et al.* (2006) (see Box 1.3) examined how much people will help others in an emergency situation (bystander intervention). They were investigating whether the degree of danger the participants considered another person to be in affected how often they helped. However, the participants were led to believe that the study was examining how men and women judge the sexual interest of the opposite sex when communicating with them (this research is described in detail in Chapter 5).

Whenever a piece of research involves deception, participants are always told about this at the end, when debriefed (Fischer *et al.* did thoroughly debrief their participants!). The participants then have the choice to withdraw their data from the analysis. Deception is always avoided where possible. Also, all research involving deception has to be approved beforehand by an ethics

Table 1.1 Summary of ethical guidelines set out by the British Psychological Society (2006)

Guideline	Description
Informed consent	Researchers must give participants information about what they will be doing so that they can agree or refuse to take part.
Deception	Misleading participants about some aspect of the research or withholding information. This can only be done if approved by an ethics committee and participants must be fully debriefed.
Debriefing	The nature and purpose of the research must be explained to the participants at the end of the research. Researchers must look out for misunderstandings or negative consequences that participants have experienced.
Right to withdraw	Participants have the right to stop taking part at any time during the research and can withdraw their data retrospectively.
Confidentiality	This is a legal requirement. All information about participants must be confidential unless otherwise agreed in advance.
Protection of participants	There must be no more risk of harm to participants than they would experience in ordinary life (including avoiding personal stress).
Observations	If people know that they are being observed, the researchers must get their consent. If the people do not know, the research must only be done in situations where people would expect to be observed by strangers anyway.
Giving advice	If a participant seeks advice, the researchers must refer them to an appropriate source of professional advice if not qualified in that area themselves.
Colleagues	Researchers share the responsibility to treat participants ethically. If a researcher believes that another is not doing their research ethically, they should encourage them to do so.

committee. You can see that psychologists do not set out to deceive people; if deception is used, it is only when necessary and the participants are informed immediately afterwards. Participants have many rights and are not helpless victims of research.

Misunderstanding four: psychology is all about hypnotizing people

Psychologists can be involved in hypnosis, but not *all* psychology or psychologists use hypnosis. Some psychologists may do research into hypnosis to examine if, when, how it works and so on (e.g. does hypnosis actually improve the recall of information about an event?). Alternatively, they may use it to help in research, such as using it to bring about a subjective experience during **brain-scanning**. It should be noted that hypnosis can only be used in research

Box 1.3 Details: referencing research

Peter Fischer, Tobias Greitemeyer, Fabian Pollozek and Dieter Frey are the psychologists doing the research. In written reports, researchers are generally referred to only by their surname (i.e. Fischer, Greitemeyer, Pollozek and Frey). As these researchers published their research in the year 2006, it is reported as Fischer, Greitemeyer, Pollozek and Frey (2006). (See Chapter 3 for more information about journals and references.)

if it has been approved ethically. Some psychologists (such as clinical or counselling psychologists) may use it in a clinical setting. Note that psychologists trained in hypnosis must still call themselves, for example, a clinical psychologist, rather than a hypnotherapist. Psychologists would certainly never use hypnosis in the way it is done on stage to entertain people.

Misunderstanding five: psychology is only about mental illness

Certain areas of psychology, such as clinical and health psychology, do deal with understanding and treating mental illnesses, and how to encourage changes in behaviour to promote good health. However, as other areas of psychology deal with people with good mental health, not *all* psychology is about mental illness.

If psychology is not all of these, then what is it? First, let's return to the list of statements. Discovering that these are not true may challenge some ideas you have always held. Yet there is evidence from psychological research which indicates that these are not true. There is evidence that hypnosis does not produce more accurate recall from memory and can actually increase the recall of incorrect information (Heap, 1988). Recordings of brain activity using **electroencephalographs** (EEGs) indicate that we do all dream every night, but we just may not always remember our dreams (Dement and Kleitman, 1957). Other evidence shows that less help is offered the more bystanders there are; that eyewitnesses' memory of an event can be inaccurate; and that brainstorming alone produces more ideas than brainstorming in groups. Such research is discussed in Chapters 5, 4 and 2 respectively. Finally, we know that we use the entire brain, not just ten per cent of it, because a specific function has been found for each part of the brain. Indeed, damage to even a small part of the brain can leave people unable to carry out specific functions (e.g. speak or move one side of the body). We can also now use **brain-imaging techniques** to watch the brain in action.

So, we know that psychology is not just using common sense, hypnosis or about mental illness. Nor does it involve reading minds or just analysing people as Freud did. In addition, psychology does not only involve self-help books which are often put in the psychology section in book shops. While self-help books are useful, they are not strictly within the realm of psychology as a discipline unless they are based on research evidence. The first piece of the puzzle about what psychology actually is, is that it uses evidence from research to verify ideas about behaviour. The list of statements also gives us the clue that psychology encompasses a diverse range of topics. The following section looks at what psychology is in more detail.

What psychology is

Psychology aims to understand the factors which lie behind the many different aspects of our behaviour. Psychology is as broad a subject as people are vastly different. For example, psychologists examine: how the brain processes language, how people behave in crowds, why we obey someone in authority, why people do or do not listen to their doctor's advice, how memory works, decision-making, personality, why an individual is prone to depression and much more.

Psychology not only investigates our behaviour, it also helps people. Zimbardo (2004) summarizes some of the ways in which psychology has made a difference to our lives. For example, psychological therapies have been developed to relieve suffering (e.g. effective treatment of panic attacks). Psychologists have shown that we can reduce discrimination and prejudice by stopping segregation in education; segregation has a negative effect on the sense of self-worth. Other research has led to a better understanding of visual perception, which in turn has led to ways to improve traffic and road safety. Also, psychologists have shown that premature babies have better growth and leave hospital earlier if they are massaged several times a day than not.

A formal definition

The word psychology comes from the Greek roots *Psyche* which means 'mind' or 'soul', and *logos* which means 'study of'. We can define psychology as:

- the systematic study of mind and behaviour;
- the scientific study of behaviour and mental processes;
- the use of experimental techniques to understand human minds and behaviour in individuals, groups and societies.

The wording may differ, but you will notice that there are common themes running through these definitions. The common themes are that psychology uses systematic or scientific methods to understand the processes going on in our minds (mental processes) and the processes underlying our behaviour (our observable behaviour and inner experiences). Also, psychology studies people at several levels: individuals, groups and whole societies. Psychology can also include study of non-human animals (e.g. chimpanzees).

The approaches and areas in psychology

Psychologists study mind and behaviour using different approaches. These different approaches are ways of explaining how we behave (including mentally). For example, biological psychology views behaviour in terms of how the body works, whereas social psychology views behaviour in terms of how people interact with each other. The range of approaches are summarized in Table 1.2. These approaches relate to the core areas in psychology. These include cognitive psychology, social psychology, developmental psychology, biological (physiological) psychology and the psychology of individual differences. We will look at each of these areas in more detail in the following chapters. None of these areas or approaches are absolutely clear-cut; there is crosstalk between them. However, they are unified by adopting a systematic and scientific approach. It should be noted that no one approach is 'correct' and psychologists can use more than one approach to study a particular topic. For example, if we take the topic of language, biological psychologists may examine which areas of our brain process different aspects of language, whereas social psychologists may study how we adapt our language when in certain groups (e.g. do you use the same type of speech when you are with your family or with your employers?).

A brief history of psychology

People's interest in understanding human behaviour has been recorded, at least, since the time of the ancient Greek philosophers, such as Aristotle and Plato. However, when considering the history of psychology as a separate 'scientific' discipline using that name, we need to look to more recent times. In Britain, the word 'psychology' was rarely used before the early 1800s and no discipline called psychology existed before the mid-nineteenth century. Psychology achieved its formal academic name in the 1880s/1890s, with the name being brought in from the word *Psychologie* used by German philosophers. Psychology's development as a distinct subject is illustrated by the publication of psychology texts and courses being offered (see Box 1.4). While some of the issues involved in psychology were studied previously (e.g. memory and visual perception were investigated since at least 1600), psychology was not recognized as a distinct discipline until it adopted experimental methods. Modern day psychology originates from the disciplines of

Table 1.2 Different approaches in psychology

Approach	Description
Cognitive	Examines the mental (cognitive) processes we use to organize and manipulate information we receive through our senses (e.g. memory, attention). Its methods include experiments and case studies of brain-damaged individuals.
Social	Concerned with how other people and the society they form influence behaviour, thoughts and emotions. It uses such methods as experiments, surveys and observations.
Developmental	Interested in how we develop over our lifespan, from conception to old age. It uses a variety of methods, such as experiments and observations.
Biological (physiological)	Examines the relationship between biological processes (e.g. the workings of the brain) and mental functions (e.g. sleep, emotion). It explores the physical basis of thoughts, feelings and behaviours. It uses a variety of methods, including experiments, observations and studying genetic versus environmental influences on behaviour.
Learning (behavioural)	Concerned with how we learn behaviours, such as associating different events with each other. It believes that most behaviour is learned and studies only observable behaviour. The learning approach takes a very scientific approach to investigation.
Evolutionary	Interested in how humans have evolved and adapted their behaviours in order to survive in their environment. It studies how inherited tendencies influence a wide range of behaviours (e.g. human reproduction).
Psychodynamic	Initially established by Freud, this approach is concerned with the influence of the unconscious mind (mental processes of which we are not normally aware). It mostly uses case studies.
Humanistic	Emphasizes the importance of the human ability to make rational, conscious choices. It values people's subjective experience as a key to understanding their behaviour. It is a non-scientific approach which proposes that we should study individuals rather than use the average performance of groups of people. It uses such techniques as flexible open-ended questions to investigate an individual's conscious experience of the world. It is primarily therapeutic.

philosophy, physiology (biology) and physics. For example, three German physiologists (Ernst Weber, Gustav Fechner and Hermann von Helmholtz) first applied experimental methods to studying psychological processes. The methods of investigation used in psychology also developed from other natural, social and mathematical subjects. Today, psychology is recognized as an established scientific discipline in its own right.

Research in psychology

The general image of science is of people in white coats doing chemistry, physics or biology experiments in laboratories. While these subjects are sciences, it is not so much the topic they examine that makes them sciences but rather the way they go about acquiring knowledge. For example, biology is a science not because it studies plants and animals, but because of the way it acquires and refines its knowledge about plants and animals. Just like biology, psychology uses **research methods** to build and refine knowledge of the way people behave and why they behave in that way. Psychology uses a variety of methods to systematically research aspects of mind and behaviour, rather than relying on common sense ideas.

All sciences share the goal of discovering knowledge using a systematic and objective method of investigation. Science can be defined as having three particular qualities; objectivity, falsifiability and replicability. Objectivity means that information is collected in such a way that feelings or opinions affect the collection as little as possible. Falsifiability means that theories can be disproved, not just proved. Replicability means that the findings of a study should be repeatable, so that theories or conclusions are not based on inconsistent findings. It is argued that psychology is not yet a fully fledged

 Box 1.4 Details: dates in psychology

- 1855 Herbert Spencer published *The Principles of Psychology*.
- 1859 Gustav Fechner published *Elements of Psychophysics*.
- 1879 Wilhelm Wundt established the first psychology laboratory in Leipzig, Germany.
- 1890 William James published *The Principles of Psychology* having begun teaching a course on the relationship between physiology and psychology at Harvard University in 1875.
- 1892 The American Psychological Association was founded.
- 1901 Psychological Society founded at University College London. The name changed to The British Psychological Society in 1906.
- 1904 Creation of the *British Journal of Psychology*.
- 1948 Creation of the *Quarterly Journal of Experimental Psychology*.
- 1959 The Experimental Psychology Group (founded in 1946) changed its name to the Experimental Psychology Society.

science, like biology or chemistry, as it possesses these qualities to varying degrees depending on which approach is considered. However, most psychology does collect evidence using particular research methods which aim to fulfil these three qualities as far as possible.

Research in psychology starts from a basic curiosity about human minds and behaviour; it may stem from ideas which spring to mind or most often lead on from previous research. Psychology does not rely on vague ideas or personal **anecdotes** as proof of a fact, but takes ideas and turns them into testable ideas or predictions (called **hypotheses**). These are then tested to obtain evidence. While there is no doubt that people's individual experiences and anecdotes are interesting, psychology is mainly concerned with the behaviour and mental processes of people *in general* and so testing is done with large numbers of people. If we tested just one person, the finding we get may relate only to that one person. That is fine if we are only interested in one person's experience, but if we want to understand human behaviour in general, then we need to know that our findings relate to most people. If we did test just one person, it could be the case that they are the 'average' person, so we would be right to assume that all people would show the same finding as them. However, they may be unusual, in which case we would incorrectly conclude that all people would behave the same as this one 'unusual' person.

Research starts with the formulation of a **theory** and specific questions or predictions (hypotheses) about a particular behaviour. To test if the theory or hypotheses are correct, psychologists can either look to facts already known or gather new evidence (some form of **data** or account) by using research methods. Psychologists use many different types of research methods, such as observing people, interviewing them, using questionnaires or doing experiments (see Chapter 2). Each method is appropriate for a variety of topics and a mixture of these methods can be used in one investigation. The information gathered is then summarized and/or analysed (using **statistics**) to show whether what has been found is a true finding or if it has happened purely by chance. The analysis indicates whether our ideas about behaviour are really true, whether they are incorrect or are **anomalies**.

Summary

This chapter has explained that psychology is the systematic study of minds and behaviour and briefly covered how psychology came to be a subject in its own right. Why and how, psychology uses a scientific approach has also been introduced. The next chapter looks at psychology research in more detail, describing different types of research methods, as well as examining the process of research and use of statistics.

2　The method behind the psychology

Chapter 2 reviews the research process, describes different research methods and explains why statistical analysis is used. It also explains the key terms used in research and gives a brief summary of some real research.

The research cycle

Psychology uses systematic methods of investigation to discover facts, as do all science subjects. Investigation can start from curiosity about something we have observed or from theories. From these theories, we make predictions. We can test these predictions by gathering data. The set of data is then summarized and/or analysed using statistics, to see whether it shows a true finding or if the finding happened by chance. If we are confident that our data is **reliable**, we then have a finding which can mean one of two things. The finding can either agree with (support) our prediction showing us that the theory is correct, or the finding may not support our prediction. If it supports our prediction, we can then test other aspects of the theory. However, if it does not support our prediction, we have to start to work out why. Maybe there was a flaw in the way we did the research? In this case, we would have to eliminate the flaw and retest the prediction. Maybe it means that the theory is not correct in the first place? In this situation, we would need to refine the theory and start testing again. This is how research goes on in a cycle.

Research methods

Psychologists find out facts about human behaviour by collecting information. The different ways of collecting information are known as research methods. The information gathered by these methods can be in a numerical form (called quantitative) that can be counted, such as the number of times a person engages in a particular behaviour. Alternatively, the information can be non-numerical (qualitative), focusing on a person's experience, such as how they feel in a certain situation. Which type of research method is used or which type of information is collected, depends on what is being examined. For example, qualitative information is more appropriate than quantitative information for some areas of human experience (e.g. individuality). Many research studies use both types of information. We now review some of the different research methods.

Surveys

Surveys, which include both questionnaires and interviews, gather information by obtaining self-report information (where people provide information about themselves). The information gathered can be quantitative (e.g. recording answers on a scale of one to seven) or qualitative (e.g. recording how participants feel about a certain issue) or both. Questionnaires are written sets of questions that people answer without the researcher having to be present. The researchers can devise their own questionnaires or use pretested ones which measure specific factors, such as a person's anxiety levels. Interviews involve having a discussion with a person and/or asking them specific questions. Interviews vary from being very structured to being free-ranging (see Table 2.1).

Surveys are a relatively quick and easy method to obtain data from large numbers of people. However, they rely on people being honest in their responses. People may give what they feel to be socially acceptable answers rather than what they really think or feel. They may fear being judged or want to give the answer they think the researcher wants to hear. In addition, people's attitudes often do not match their behaviour, so the data cannot always predict what people will do. A limitation of clinical interviews (a face to face interview where a person provides information about their problems) is that it is difficult to compare one person's data to another's. Case studies, which are essentially an interview with one person, gather a lot of detailed information but this one person's data cannot be applied to all other people.

Observations

Observations involve watching and recording people's naturally occurring behaviour (Table 2.2 details types of observations). The behaviours are coded using a scheme worked out by the researchers. Generally, more than one person observes so that the findings are not biased by just one person's interpretation of the behaviour. The data from the two observers is compared to see how well they agree (there should be fairly good agreement for the data to be reliable). This is called **inter-observer reliability**. An advantage of

Table 2.1 Types of survey

Type	Description
Fully-structured interview	The interviewer asks all participants the same questions in the same order. The participants select their answers from a limited set of specific answers (e.g. yes, no).
Non-directive (unstructured) interview	Participants and interviewer can discuss anything that they want to, with no restrictions on questions asked or answers given.
Informal interview	The interviewer directs the interview by exploring certain topics rather than being non-directive, but participants are free to discuss anything they wish to within these topics.
Guided (semi-structured) interview	The interviewer asks all participants the same questions in the same order but the answers can be open-ended. It is more structured than an informal interview.
Clinical interview	This is similar to a guided interview. The same questions are given to all participants but the choice of follow-up questions depends on the answers given. Later questions are based on answers to earlier questions.
Questionnaire surveys	These are in a written format and vary in how specific or free-ranging they are. Psychological tests in questionnaire format are standardized for a population and checked for validity and reliability (e.g. intelligence tests). Opinion surveys can have **open-ended** or **closed questions**.

Table 2.2 Types of observation

Type	Description
Naturalistic	Records spontaneously occurring behaviour in the participants' natural environment.
Participant	Researcher becomes involved in, and records, the day-to-day life of the participants, with or without them knowing.
Controlled	Researcher records spontaneously occurring behaviour but in conditions which they have set up (e.g. in a laboratory).

observations is that they are done in natural settings and so have high **ecological validity** (that is, they reflect behaviours that occur in real world situations to a high degree). They can also be used to generate further research or validate findings from other research. Their disadvantages include not being able to **control** factors which could negatively affect the behaviour or data, and ethical problems with gaining consent or debriefing participants (see Table 1.1 in Chapter 1).

Correlational analysis

Correlational analysis is where researchers study the link between two particular factors, looking for associations between them (e.g. examining the link between **genetics** and **extraversion**). The analysis indicates whether a relationship exists, whether the relationship is positive or negative, and how strong it is on a scale of –1 to +1. A positive correlation is where two factors are related so that large values of one factor are associated with large values of another factor (e.g. parent's high intelligence associated with child's high intelligence). A negative correlation is where large values of one factor are associated with small values of the second factor (e.g. the more hours a child spends playing computer games, the shorter their attention span). A perfect positive correlation is shown as +1, whereas a perfect negative correlation is shown as –1. No correlation means that there is no association between the two factors; they are unrelated (shown as a value of 0). An advantage of using correlations is that the researchers do not need to manipulate any behaviour. A limitation is that they cannot establish cause and effect; it cannot show if one factor is *causing* changes in the other, just that they are associated.

Longitudinal and cross-sectional studies

Longitudinal research involves studying the same people over a period of time (e.g. several years). This method is particularly popular for studying people's development. A disadvantage of longitudinal studies is that any improvements over time could be due to practise (e.g. on completing a questionnaire), rather than true developmental factors. They also take a lot of time, and some participants may stop taking part. Development can also be studied using a cross-sectional technique, which compares the behaviour of different age groups at a set time, such as comparing how a set of 4-year-olds and a set of 10-year-olds perform on a test. However, this cannot compare the same individuals as they develop over time, so any differences in behaviour may arise from differences in these people rather than from differences due to development. This is not a problem for longitudinal studies.

Experimental method

The experimental method involves manipulating one factor to see what effect it has on another factor (e.g. how ingesting caffeine affects memory for words). Table 2.3 shows the variations of this method. Experiments are often done in

Table 2.3   Variations of the experimental method

Variation	Description and evaluation
Laboratory experiment	This is conducted in a controlled setting. The experimenter manipulates the independent variable while strictly controlling the environment to prevent extraneous variables therefore affecting the procedure. It has high **internal validity** and objectivity, participants can be fully debriefed. It has low ecological validity.
Field experiment	This is the same as a laboratory experiment, but done in the participant's natural setting rather than in a laboratory. It has high ecological validity but less control over extraneous variables. It can be difficult to replicate and to record data accurately. It is hard to debrief participants.
Natural/quasi-experiment	An experiment where the researchers cannot control the independent variable because it occurs naturally (e.g. gender, having brain damage). It has greater ecological validity than other methods but researchers have less control than a laboratory experiment. Participants cannot be randomly allocated to different groups. It can be difficult to replicate and to debrief participants.

a controlled setting so that unwanted factors, called **extraneous variables**, cannot affect behaviour (e.g. noise, influences from other people). Using a controlled setting also means that all participants experience nearly the same thing. Experiments have the advantage, they can establish cause and effect relationships through having a lot of control over the events and factors that are being manipulated. One disadvantage is that experiments tend to be done in an artificial setting, not in a real world setting. Experiments are also not suitable for some topics. Experiments necessarily focus on a narrow range of factors, but in doing so they may miss other factors that are also involved in the behaviour being studied.

Case studies

A case study method is used to obtain information about a single individual or a group of people. This method can involve interviewing, observing or testing one person (or group). Case studies are used in research particularly where unusual examples of behaviour can provide insights into theories or psychological processes. For instance, case studies of brain-damaged individuals are used in **neuropsychology** to examine how particular parts of the brain relate to particular behaviours. Case studies have the advantage of providing a lot of in-depth and detailed information about one person. However, they are difficult to **replicate** and it is not easy to relate the findings from one person to the population in general. Case studies are also used in therapy (e.g. in Freud's psychodynamic approach).

Meta-analysis

In a meta-analysis, the researchers do not actually recruit people to take part in an investigation; they use previous research on a specific topic instead. Meta-analysis is a technique which pulls together a large collection of research findings from individual studies, codes their findings and then interprets them to arrive at one 'overall' result. It is useful for just about any area in psychology and has the advantage of giving an overview of a particular issue.

Discourse (content) analysis

Discourse analysis is a method which examines the way that the language we use (discourse) effects how we interpret our social world. This includes language in its spoken and written forms. Discourse analysis aims to uncover hidden meanings in our language, such as language which promotes certain attitudes (e.g. prejudice). It involves analysing speech/writing, using a set of criteria in order to record the data as units (e.g. individual words), and categorizing these units into groups. The advantage of this method is that it can show how language affects people's views and, it can aim to alter language to stop promoting, for example, prejudiced views. However, in a discourse it is hard to separate the influence of factors outside of a person (e.g. social influences) from the influence of factors within a person (e.g. from their upbringing).

Summary of research methods

The research methods mentioned above are not an exhaustive list but they do show the variety of methods available. These research methods are all useful and no one technique is considered more 'correct' than another. Which method is used depends on whether the researchers are looking for relationships between factors or whether one factor causes changes in another. The experimental method is claimed to be the most objective way of collecting data, whereas other methods (e.g. discourse analysis) allow for more subjective information to be collected. The research methods vary in how they perform a balancing act between controlling all factors for objectivity and sacrificing control for other advantages, such as higher ecological validity. In addition, the practicalities of doing the research can also influence the choice of research method. For example, if you want to use questionnaires, do you have access to large numbers of people? Of course, the issue of being ethical applies to all research methods.

Key terms in research

There are some key terms used in research which you need to know. To introduce them, we will run through an imaginary experiment and look at them as they appear (key terms are in italics). Although we are looking at one research method (an experiment), these terms are applicable to all research methods.

Caffeine and memory

Imagine that we have a *theory* that drinking coffee when studying affects our ability to remember that information later on. There are several aspects of our theory which could be tested: does drinking coffee really improve our performance? Is it the caffeine in the coffee that affects our performance or would any hot drink do? Does just thinking that it has an effect improve our performance? As we cannot test all aspects in one go (it would involve far too many different factors), we **aim** to only test whether drinking caffeinated coffee affects our ability to remember information.

We first need to decide on one specific question or prediction to test, called the *hypothesis*. A hypothesis is a clear statement about what we believe is true, according to our theory. Our hypothesis will be 'drinking caffeinated coffee will affect people's ability to remember unfamiliar words'. As you can see, the hypothesis is quite specific (e.g. remembering unfamiliar words, not just words). This is our *experimental hypothesis* (annotated as H_1). We state this hypothesis with the aim of proving or disproving it. As our experimental hypothesis simply states that there will be a difference, as in 'drinking caffeinated coffee will affect people's ability . . .' it is a **non-directional hypothesis**. A **directional hypothesis** would state the direction in which we predict the effect to occur (e.g. 'drinking caffeinated coffee will improve people's ability to remember unfamiliar words'). We also need to state a **null hypothesis** (H_0). Our null hypothesis is 'drinking caffeinated coffee will not affect people's ability to remember unfamiliar words'. The null hypothesis relates to the situation where our findings happen by chance.

The experimental and null hypotheses both specify two important factors. The first is the **variable** (factor that changes) which we are going to manipulate, called the **independent variable**, and the second is the variable which may be affected by this manipulation, called the **dependent variable**. In an investigation, the researcher manipulates the independent variable (IV) to see if it causes changes in the dependent variable (DV). While the researcher controls the IV, the DV is free to change. The researcher measures changes in the

DV. In our experiment, the independent variable will be whether we drink caffeinated coffee or not. The dependent variable will be the performance of recalling unfamiliar words. The dependent variable is the one which we will be measuring, so we can liken it to the data we will be collecting. If we were doing a correlational analysis instead of an experiment, we would predict a relationship between two factors instead of a difference (e.g. 'the more hours a person works in a week, the higher their levels of stress').

How would we actually go about manipulating the IV in our imaginary experiment? The first step is to decide on the different *levels* that we will use for the IV. We will have people drinking caffeinated coffee and not drinking caffeinated coffee. These relate to the two **conditions** of the IV. When we actually do the experiment, we will have one group of people in one condition who drink caffeinated coffee (caffeine condition) and another group in another condition who do not drink caffeinated coffee (no-caffeine condition). The people in the no-caffeine condition will drink decaffeinated coffee, rather than having no drink at all, as we want to make sure that the people in both conditions are having as similar an experience as possible apart from the factor we are manipulating. The condition which we expect contains the critical factor is called the **experimental condition**. In our case, this is the caffeine condition as we suspect that caffeine affects the ability to recall information. The condition which we expect does not contain the critical factor is the **control condition**. In our case, this is the no-caffeine condition. Next, we need to decide what the dependent variable(s) will be. There can be several ways of measuring this and any research can use one or more different measures. In our case, the DV(s) will be the measure(s) of the people's ability to recall unfamiliar words.

There are other factors which we must consider before we can actually start doing the experiment. These relate to the people who will take part and the way we do our experiment. First, let's consider the people from whom we will be obtaining data. As we are studying psychology, we invariably need people to take part in our experiment! Aside from the practicalities of getting people to take part, we need to consider their characteristics and how these might affect our findings. This applies to all research methods, not just experiments.

We select our participants from a **population**. The population is all of the members of a particular group. A population can correspond to geography (e.g. every adult in the country) or to a category where they all share a feature, such as all people who smoke. The population for our experiment could be all people within a certain age band that do not normally drink caffeinated coffee. However, we cannot test every single adult in this group in the country. What we need is a small selection of that population, a **sample**, which represents the population, in that they share the same characteristics and the full range of diversity in that population. The way we select our participants is *sampling*. There are different methods of sampling (see Table 2.4). When people are aware that they are being selected, they are called a volunteer sample. We need to be careful to not use a sample which does not represent the population or is biased in some way. Having a representative sample is important as it will allow you to **generalize** your findings from the sample back to the whole population. Equally, we must try to do research so that it is not biased to one gender or culture.

People can affect the findings of a piece of research, by bringing their expectations to the experiment or from the effects of just taking part (known as *participant reactivity*). We need to be aware of these effects and rule them out or control them. This includes participants being nervous about taking part and/or anxious about being evaluated (*evaluation apprehension*). Another aspect that must be considered is the presence of *demand characteristics*, which is where the participant works out what the research study is examining and what is being expected of them, and alters their behaviour to please the researcher or spoil the study. They may guess the aim from clues they pick up and alter their behaviour deliberately or without realizing. One way to get around this problem is to keep the amount of information they know about the study to a minimum, until they have finished or to use deception by telling them it is about something else. A **single-blind** method, where the participants do not know which condition they are in, is effective. There is also the problem of *experimenter expectancy*, where the experimenter (consciously or unconsciously) influences the results to achieve the desired outcome of the research. A **double-blind** technique should then be used, which is where neither the researcher, nor the participants, know the aim of the research or the conditions they are in.

Before we start our experiment we must also consider the way we will do our experiment. We need to decide on, and prepare, any **materials** or **apparatus** that we will use (e.g. we will need caffeinated and decaffeinated

Table 2.4 Some sampling methods

Sampling method	Description
Random sampling	When every person in a population has an equal chance of being selected (e.g. by pulling names out of a hat).
Systematic sampling	Where people are selected at set intervals (e.g. using every tenth person out of a population).
Quota sampling	Where the population is divided into representative subgroups (strata) from which quotas are taken in the same proportion as they occur in the population, by whatever means is convenient.
Opportunity sampling	Selecting people that are around and available at that time.

coffee, a set of unfamiliar words, etc.). When setting-up the experiment, it is very important, to choose materials/apparatus that are suitable tests for the hypothesis and which do actually measure what they are supposed to measure. The extent to which a method measures, what it aims to measure, is known as **validity**. We also need to consider *reliability*, which is whether we would get the same findings if we did an exact **replication** of this experiment. In fact, the written report of the research should be as detailed as possible so that someone who knows nothing about the research investigation should be able to replicate it. Reliability and validity affect how well the results will generalize to the whole population. *Ecological validity* refers to how well the research is measuring behaviour as it would occur in a natural setting. We also need to consider how we are going to keep unwanted factors (extraneous variables) from affecting people's behaviour and our results. For instance, we need to consider whether people's different coffee drinking habits would affect the results and, we would need to use words unfamiliar to everyone in the study (possibly from a foreign language or nonsense words). Also, we must give all participants the same, standardized instructions: they must be treated in exactly the same way.

The next consideration is how we allocate people into the two conditions. All of the participants could experience both conditions, which would be a **within-participants design**. Or the people could only experience one condition, so that different people were in each condition, which is a **between-participants design**. Each design has its strengths and limitations. For instance, having all participants do all conditions (within-participants) rules out the effect of individual differences between people but it also introduces fatigue, boredom, or becoming practised at a task (called **order effects**). This can be avoided by **counterbalancing** the order in which they do the different conditions, so that half of the people do the caffeine condition first and half do the no-caffeine condition first. On the other hand, having people do just one condition (between-participants) introduces the unwanted effect of any differences between individuals affecting the results but rules out order effects. The researchers judge which design is most appropriate, bearing their strengths and limitations in mind.

We would now be ready to do the experiment and collect the data. We may first run a *pilot study* (a small-scale version) to test its reliability and iron out any problems, before doing the full investigation. Of course, we would follow all ethical guidelines. The sets of data from the full investigation will be analysed (using statistical tests) to see what they show and so that we can draw conclusions about what we have found.

Why use statistics?

In our imaginary experiment, we would have collected two sets of data; one from the caffeine condition and one from the no-caffeine condition. Once collected, these sets can be summarized to give such information as **averages** and how much the data vary around the average. The data can also be represented graphically (e.g. bar charts). These are called descriptive statistics. According to our experimental hypothesis, we expect to find a difference in ability to recall unfamiliar words between the conditions. To work this out, we need to use descriptive statistics and to analyse the data using statistics. What type of data we have collected (e.g. measurements, ratings), how we allocated participants into conditions, and what we are looking for (relationships or differences) determines which kind of statistical test will be used. We will not explain all of the possible statistical tests here, as they are a textbook in itself, but we will look at *why* they are used (a variety of tests will be introduced in the core area chapters where we look at real research papers).

Inferential statistics are used to tell us how **significant** our results are. Significance does not just mean that the results are important; it refers to the likelihood that the difference in behaviour did happen due to our manipulation of the IV and not due to chance. That is, is the difference between the conditions real or is it just a fluke of the experiment this time? To know whether our results are significant, we use a statistical test to work out how likely (probable) it is that the data occurred by chance. The benchmark is generally the level of equal to, or less than, five per cent **probability** that the results occurred due to chance factors (i.e. 1 in 20). If our data's level of probability is equal to/less than five per cent, then we can conclude that our finding is significant and is most likely due to our manipulation of the IV. We would then report our results are significant at the probability of less than/equal to five per cent (written as $p < 0.05$). Some research uses more stringent levels, such as $p < 0.001$ (i.e. 1 in 1000 probability that they arose by chance). However, if there is more than a five per cent probability that the results did happen by chance, we conclude that we have not found any evidence (the result probably happened by coincidence). If our analysis showed that there is a significant difference between the two conditions, then we can *reject* our null hypothesis, which means that we have found support for our experimental hypothesis. If the analysis does not show a significant difference, then we must *accept* our null hypothesis.

The imaginary experiment on how drinking caffeinated coffee affects memory, has introduced the key terms used in research. As mentioned before, doing an experiment is not the only method of research, but it does allow for the introduction of terms which are common in research. You can see how these concepts and terms are used in a piece of real research in Box 2.1.

Box 2.1 Research: does group brainstorming work?

It is known from previous research that people **brainstorming** alone generate more ideas than groups. Despite this, over 80 per cent of people still think that brainstorming in groups is more effective than working as an individual. Nijstad, Stroebe and Lodewijkx reported the results of three experiments in the *European Journal of Social Psychology* in 2006. They questioned why people feel happier with their performance of producing ideas when they brainstorm in a group than when alone, even though they produce fewer ideas. Their theory is that people working in groups do not notice their failures to produce new ideas as much as people working alone. As they perceive fewer failures, they feel that their output is more satisfactory. To test this, they conducted three separate experiments to test three different (but related) ideas. We will concentrate here on their first experiment which tested the hypothesis that people in groups experience fewer failures, and so feel more satisfied, than individuals working alone.

How did they do this?
They allocated 122 participants (56 male, 66 female) into groups (of four or six people), dyads (two-person groups) or working alone (individuals). They were all given the task of thinking of ways that they could increase the number of tourists visiting Utrecht (The Netherlands). All were given the same instructions. They were then taken to separate rooms to do the task. Each room had a table with a microphone in the middle (so the researchers could record them). The group/dyad/person decided when to stop the task. They then completed a questionnaire which measured their satisfaction with their performance, how difficult they found it to keep on coming up with ideas, how often they failed to create new ideas and how often they came up with ideas which had already been generated. For instance, they rated satisfaction with their own performance on a scale of one to nine. The researchers then debriefed the participants and the experiment ended.

What did they find?
Nijstad *et al.* (2006) analysed the data that they had collected. For example, for the satisfaction data, they looked at whether there was a difference in ratings of satisfaction between the groups, dyads and individuals. They found that group members, whether in groups or dyads, felt more satisfied with their production of ideas than the individuals working alone. In addition, the individuals experienced more failures than groups or dyads. The data supported their hypothesis.

What does this investigation show us about psychology research?

- It illustrates some of the key concepts in research: it shows that they have a theory and hypothesis; they used a between-participants design, allocating participants into groups, dyads or alone conditions; they collected quantitative data (e.g. participants rated their satisfaction on a scale); they followed ethical procedures by debriefing the participants; and the data supported their hypothesis.
- It investigates a topic in the area of social psychology. This area explains behaviour in terms of the way people interact with each other (see Table 1.2 in Chapter 1).
- It shows the use of one type of research method, a laboratory experiment. The experiment was done in a room, rather than outside in the 'real world'.
- It shows how certain factors were controlled. For example, they used standardized procedures, giving all participants the same task instructions. They also controlled the number of males and females in a group so that it was equal (i.e. a group of six had three males and three females). This is important as all-male groups may interact differently from all-female groups, which could affect the results. Also, this research was not specifically interested in the effect of gender, so balancing the numbers of males and females controls this factor as a possible extraneous variable.

The effect of caffeine on memory has actually been, and is being, researched. It has been found, for example, that people recall pairs of words better if they drink a caffeinated drink while learning them *and* while recalling them (Kelemen and Creeley, 2003). However, the overall evidence for the effect of caffeine on memory is somewhat mixed.

Summary

In this chapter, we have looked at the research process used to examine human behaviour and some of the methods used to do this research. The key terms in research and why statistics are used have been introduced by looking at an imaginary experiment. These are also illustrated in the summary of a real piece of research (Box 2.1). The next chapter moves on to how psychologists report and share their findings from such research.

3 How psychological research is reported

Psychologists use a variety of research methods to examine people's mental processes and behaviour. In this chapter, we look at how such research is written and where it is published. We will look at the way a piece of research is reported and then look at a real research paper. This research investigates how quickly and accurately people can recognize something that is threatening, which is an important part of how we act in a dangerous situation.

Reporting research in psychology

Having a written report of a piece of research is important for two reasons. First, it enables other people and psychologists to read about it. This is an essential part of psychology because we need to share and discuss findings in order for knowledge to advance. For example, the research may be testing a particular theory, and it is useful for other psychologists to know if there is evidence to support this theory. Second, it means that we can assess the findings. If psychologist X has done an experiment, how do we know how good the findings are unless psychologist Y can read about them, and maybe test them himself/herself? It is also important for the research to be available so that other researchers can try to replicate the study.

How do psychologists write about and publish their research?

Psychologists tend to have (at least!) one thing in common; they have learnt about the different areas of psychology, how to do research and how to write their findings as a report. In psychology, we commonly call such a report a 'research paper' or 'article'. Most psychologists will do some research as part of their job. As research is done to test ideas and find ways to improve people's lives, it would be of no use for psychologists to keep these findings to themselves. To share their findings, they write them up as a research paper and submit it to a psychology journal (see Box 3.1). Each submission to a journal is scrutinized by a panel of other psychologists who will provide feedback on it. Not every paper is accepted to be published; the reviewers may decide that it is not good enough, or will only be once it has been revised. The process of being scrutinized by other psychologists is called **peer review**. Once it is accepted, the research paper will be published in the latest issue of the journal. In a journal, nearly all papers are written in the same format.

Why do you need to know about the format?

Writing up research is not just for working psychologists. Anyone studying psychology, whether at school, university or in an adult education setting, will not just read about research but may have to write a report. For instance, A level psychology requires each student to conduct and report a research study. Understanding the format will not only show you how it is written, but will also help you to understand the research methods used.

The basic format of a research paper

All research papers follow a set structure with the same specific sections in the same order. These sections tell the story of the research. They describe what the researchers did, why and how they did it, what was found and what it means. The research paper will also always have a reference section which lists other

---

 Box 3.1 Details: what is a journal?

A journal is a collection of research papers. Traditionally, these are bound together like a book and printed at certain intervals (e.g. quarterly) as issues. Several issues are eventually bound together to form one volume of a journal, which looks a bit like an encyclopaedia. Nowadays, journals are also available online. A current issue, or volume of a journal, has the latest research happening in psychology. Journals are stocked in university and college libraries, or you can subscribe to them. There are hundreds of psychology journals published world-wide, each of which specializes in a certain area of psychology. The list below shows just a few journals, but illustrates the variety available.

- *Quarterly Journal of Experimental Psychology*
- *Journal of Social Psychology*
- *Journal of Experimental Child Psychology*
- *Legal and Criminological Psychology*
- *Journal of Health Psychology.*

papers and books that the researchers have referred to in the paper. Sometimes (but not always) the paper will include appendices. We will look at each of these sections in turn.

The title

All research papers have a title. The title is very important as it is the first thing that the reader sees and uses to decide whether to read on further. As such, the title should be as informative about the topic of the paper as possible. If the title is of interest, and looks like it will be relevant reading, the reader will then go on to look at the abstract for more information.

The abstract

The abstract is the first section of a paper. It is a short paragraph which summarizes what the paper is about. It outlines the bare bones of the research by describing what topic was examined, what was expected to be found, what was done, what was actually found and what was concluded.

The introduction

The introduction is like the beginning of the story; it sets the scene for the rest of the paper. The introduction is written in more detail than the abstract. In general, it is an account of the reasons why the research is being done and what it is about. The introduction begins by describing and discussing other research that has already been done on this particular subject. It explains what the existing research tells us and why there is a need for further research. It then moves on to explain why this particular research is being done. It ends with the aims of the research and the hypotheses that are being tested. So, it begins in a broad way and then gradually focuses on the research being reported.

The method

The method describes exactly what happened in the research. It describes this in enough detail that anyone else could do the exact same research again (i.e. replicate it). It should be noted that a piece of research can include more than one investigation (e.g. involving three experiments). The method has its own subsections; the design, participants, apparatus and/or materials and procedure sections.

- The *design* section explains how the investigation was set up (e.g. defining what the conditions are). What this section explains will become clearer when we look at an actual paper.
- The *participants* section describes the people who took part (it used to be called 'subjects'). It can describe such characteristics as gender, age, how they were sampled and so on.

- The *apparatus/materials* section describes any equipment used. 'Apparatus' refers to items, such as computers, whereas 'materials' refers to such items as paper, word lists, questionnaires and so on.
- The *procedure* section describes, in chronological order, exactly what happened in the investigation. It is a step by step account of what happened to the participant(s) from start to finish.

The results

This section reports the findings by describing the information collected and the results of any statistical analysis. For example, it may report the averages of the data and whether the findings are due to chance or are real (significant) findings. This section often uses tables and graphs.

The discussion

The discussion is the end of the story. It rounds off the research paper by interpreting and explaining what was found. It first outlines the results and states whether the data supports the hypotheses. It then discusses what the results mean. For instance, do these findings agree with other theories or research that has been done? The discussion also considers whether further research needs doing.

The reference section

The reference section lists all sources of information (e.g. research papers, books) mentioned (cited) in the research paper. This section is important as it acknowledges the work of others and enables readers to locate this information themselves. As with the format of a research paper, references are always written in a set way (see Box 3.2).

 Box 3.2 Details: the reference section

The reference section is always written in a set format. In psychology, the reference section is usually listed in alphabetical order by author surname. Each reference to a book or research paper is then written in a conventional way, beginning with author surname, initial, year of publication, title and so on (look at the reference section at the end of this book to see how these are done). The exact format depends on which referencing system is being used; these have slight differences and preferences. This book uses the Harvard system. The system set out by the American Psychological Association is also common in psychology.

Appendices

Sometimes an appendix, or several appendices, appear at the end of the paper. These present information that cannot be included in the main paper. For example, the investigation may have used a questionnaire that would be too long to be included in the main paper, but will be of enough interest to be included as an appendix.

Research paper

You should now have some idea of the sections that are included in a research paper. We will now look at an actual research paper to examine how these sections are written. The research paper used here was written by Tipples, Young, Quinlan, Broks and Ellis, and published in 2002 (as is conventional, the full reference is in the reference section at the end of this book). They report a series of five experiments, but we will look at just one of these. Before looking at the format, we will explore the background to the research.

Background: detecting threat and visual search

Consider the scenario where you are walking along and a snarling dog suddenly appears from behind a gate. How do you respond? One possibility is that you will very quickly realize that the dog is potentially harmful and take action by running away. On the other hand, you could (recklessly) stand still for some time, considering what you are seeing and whether it is dangerous. The chances are that you will have moved away from the dog, before you realize what is happening. The research paper by Tipples *et al.* (2002) focuses on one part of this scenario: how good we are at detecting something that is threatening. They conducted five experiments to investigate whether we are faster and more accurate at detecting something that is threatening than non-threatening. It makes sense for us to be good at detecting a threat, such as a snarling dog, as it helps us to survive or go unharmed. Indeed, our brains seem to be tuned to recognize something as a threat more rapidly and accurately than something that is not a threat. Tipples *et al.* (2002) refer to this tuning as showing 'preferential processing' for threatening **stimuli**.

One idea is that all people show preferential processing for threatening things. An alternative idea is that only certain people have this ability, such as people with high anxiety or phobias (known as clinical groups). Some previous research shows that clinical groups are especially good at detecting threat. However, Tipples *et al.* (2002) think that the clinical groups' high ability to detect threatening stimuli, is just an exaggeration of something that exists in all of us. They test this by investigating whether everyone (the general population) can process threatening stimuli rapidly and accurately (i.e. preferentially). They examine this by seeing whether the general population can detect a picture of something threatening more quickly and accurately than a picture of something non-threatening.

Tipples *et al.* (2002) use a method called 'visual search' (also known as the visual search paradigm). Imagine that you are looking for your sister's face in a large crowd of people. Your sister's face is the 'target' item that you are looking for and you will recognize it because it has certain features. All the other faces in the crowd are 'distractors'. They may look similar to your sister's face, as they share some features (all have two eyes, a nose, etc.), but they are not your target. Visual search is the process of visually checking through these distractor faces until you spot your target face. You may have to check each item in turn because there is too much information (too many faces) to look at, all at the same time. If a target is spotted very quickly and accurately, we can conclude that it has some significance for us. It might be something that our brain is tuned to be vigilant for and so it catches our attention. If it captures our attention, regardless of how many distractors are around, then it is said to 'pop-out'. Box 3.3 explains how psychologists do a visual search experiment. In their visual search experiment, Tipples *et al.* (2002) use pictures of animals and plants. The animals are the threatening stimuli, and the plants are the non-

---

 Box 3.3 Methods: visual search

Psychologists use a visual search method in experiments by presenting a display of items on a computer screen and asking the participant to search for a particular item. This particular item is known as the target. The participant presses a designated key on the keyboard depending on whether they can see the target or not. A computer programme records which keys are pressed and how fast, indicating how accurately and quickly the participant detects if the target is there or not.

In a typical visual search experiment, participants search for a target item among a background of distractors. The target may be something like a red O among blue Os and red Xs. Sometimes the target is there (called target present trials) and sometimes the target is missing (called target absent trials). The participants see displays of targets and distractors many times. The number of distractors in the displays varies (e.g. displays may have four, eight or twelve distractors).

It is generally found that certain targets can be spotted quickly and accurately, regardless of the amount of distractors in the displays (they pop-out), whereas it becomes harder to find other types of targets as the number of distractors increases. Pop-out happens when we can visually process these types of stimuli automatically.

threatening stimuli. They use pictures of animals, such as bears, dogs and snakes, which are considered to be threatening as they are ready to attack. All the animals have open mouths and the dogs and bears have exposed teeth. The participants see displays of an animal target among plant distractors and vice versa.

We will now turn to the research paper by Tipples *et al.* (2002) in order to look at the format of a paper. The paper is mostly reprinted as it actually is; some material is not included but this is purely for brevity or simplicity. The actual words are used to give you a feel for the type of language used. In some places I have inserted my own words, which are in square brackets (i.e. [ ]). The content of the paper is presented in segments. Each segment is followed by a commentary underneath which explains what type of information is contained in that segment. The paper also introduces you to a research method. Do not worry if you do not yet understand all the terms, just focus on the type of information in each section.

The paper

Tipples, J., Young, A.W., Quinlan, P., Broks, P. and Ellis, A.W. (2002) Searching for threat, *The Quarterly Journal of Experimental Psychology*, 55A(3): 1007–26.

This is the title (and is also how this research paper is written as a reference). It lists the five authors and the year it was published. It shows the title of their research paper (Searching for threat), and then lists the journal it is published in (*The Quarterly Journal* . . .), the volume number (55A), issue number (3) and pages (1007–1026).

Abstract

A visual search task was used to test the idea that biologically relevant threatening stimuli might be recognized very quickly . . . In Experiment 1, there was evidence for both faster detection and faster search rates for threatening animals than for plants . . . We conclude [from the whole series of experiments] that the visual search paradigm does not readily reveal any biases that might exist for threatening stimuli in the general population.

The abstract summarizes what method was used (i.e. a visual search task) and states what hypothesis (idea) is being examined. It states what was found and what the authors conclude from the whole series of five experiments. This section does not go into detail as it is a summary of what was done.

Introduction

The idea that threatening stimuli are recognized especially quickly . . . continues to appeal to psychologists (Mogg and Bradley, 1998; Öhman, Flykt and Lundqvist, 1999). From an evolutionary viewpoint, the efficient detection of threatening stimuli confers obvious survival value . . . The hypothesis of preferential processing of threat stimuli can be considered applicable to all individuals in the population, or only to certain groups (highly anxious people, phobics, and so on). A substantial literature attests to the presence of biases in the processing of threat stimuli in relevant clinical groups (Bradley, Mogg, White, Groom, and de Bono, 1999) but our concern here is with the idea that these clinical biases are simply exaggerated forms of a tendency present in everyone. This is of interest because evolutionary and **neurophysiological** perspectives have been used to imply that it is an **intrinsic** property of brain organization that threatening stimuli will receive preferential processing. That is the hypothesis we investigate here. The current study tests the notion that threat stimuli are processed automatically and efficiently, or capture visual attention. Specifically, we . . . [use] a visual search task to test this hypothesis.

The introduction begins by 'setting the scene' as it states what the paper is interested in. The introduction discusses the idea that all people in the population may be 'tuned' to recognize a threat efficiently, or only certain groups of people are, such as those with phobias. The authors then refer to research that has been already done on this topic (called 'literature'). They hypothesize that the tendency to detect threat is not just present in clinical groups but is present in everyone. The authors then move on to describe the method they will use.

The visual search task has been used to examine visual search for evolutionary-relevant stimuli. For example, Öhman et al. (1999) asked participants to search through arrays of fear-irrelevant pictures (flowers, mushrooms) and fear-relevant pictures (snakes and spiders). In support of the evolutionary hypothesis, participants were faster to detect a snake or a spider among flowers or mushrooms than vice versa . . . fear-relevant targets were detected more quickly and seemed to exhibit pop-out. Experiment 1 focused on producing a replication of the pattern of findings discussed by Öhman et al. (1999). Participants were asked to search for animals or plants. All animal stimuli were pictured making threatening gestures (e.g. snarling with bared teeth). Responding quickly to such gestures has long been thought of as an important evolutionary adaptation (Darwin, 1872). Following Öhman et al. (1999), we predicted faster overall decisions for threatening stimuli . . . with reduced or near zero search rates for threatening stimuli compared to plants . . .

The visual search method has been used before for this topic, so this is a form of replication of a previous study by Öhman *et al.* (1999). The target is the item that the participants are required to specifically search for. The authors describe the aim of Experiment 1, how it was done and what they predict will be found. A search rate refers to how quickly a participant detects an item as the number of distractors increases. A near zero search rate indicates that something can be detected very quickly and accurately regardless of the number of distractors present.

Method

Participants
A total of 12 psychology students (5 male, 7 female) from the University of York took part in return for a course credit.

Stimuli and apparatus
All 12 stimuli were coloured photographs of animals poised to attack (e.g. snakes, bears and dogs). Of these, 10 were selected from the International **Affective** Picture System . . . all the animal pictures were rated for valence on a 9-point scale (1 = unpleasant, 9 = pleasant) and arousal on a 9-point scale (1 = completely relaxed, 9 = completely aroused). The **mean** ratings show that the animal pictures chosen for Experiment 1, were perceived as arousing (M = 6.34, SD = 0.42) and unpleasant (M = 3.88, SD = 0.28). The remaining two animal images were selected from other sources of wildlife photography . . . The plant pictures included a mixture of leaves and flowers. Each picture was cropped to fit a screen window area measuring 89 mm [millimetre] wide . . . × 79 mm deep . . . Stimuli were presented on a 19-inch . . . monitor. Each participant sat 80 cm away from the computer monitor.

Design
The main experiment consisted of 192 trials. These trials were split into four equal blocks, according to whether the target was an animal or plant, using ABBA or BAAB orders that were counterbalanced across participants. Within each block, 24 of the trials involved searching for targets in four picture arrays (12 target-present, 12 target-absent trials) and 24 trials involved searching for targets in nine picture arrays (12 target-present, 12 target-absent trials) . . . Trial order was randomized.

The method has four subsections: participants, stimuli and apparatus, design and procedure. The participants section reports the total number of participants and how this breaks down into gender. A lot of psychology research uses students as their participants. Most degree courses require students to take part for credits which count towards their mark. This supplies a 'pool' of readily available participants and the students experience many different types of methods. As well as listing the apparatus used (the type of computer), this paper also describes the stimuli used in detail. The stimuli take the place of the materials here. The stimuli details are necessary so that other researchers could replicate this experiment exactly. It describes what the stimuli were (the pictures used). It also explains where these came from (the International Affective Picture System is a catalogue of suitable pictures). The animal pictures were rated for their valence (how attractive/repulsive they are) and arousal (how much they stimulated emotion in the viewer). This means that not only do the researchers know how 'threatening' they are, but someone replicating this experiment could find similar pictures of the same level of valence and arousal. The 'M' stands for mean and the 'SD' stands for **standard deviation**. It then describes the plant pictures in equal detail. The size of the pictures as they appear on the computer screen is important, as if some participants saw the pictures much smaller or larger than others, this could affect the findings (this would be an extraneous variable; see Chapter 2). This is also the reason why the authors mention how far the participants sat from the computer monitor.

The design section explains how the experiment is structured. It mentions what groups the participants were put in, how the stimuli were allocated to each participant and so on. Tipples *et al.* (2002) explain that there are 192 trials (displays) that appear on the computer screen. Half of these displays are where the target is an animal, and half where the target is a plant. These animal and plant groups are then split in half again, to make four blocks. The authors describe the order these are seen in. For example, ABBA means that the participants saw animal targets, then plants, plants again then animals. 'Counterbalanced' means that all orders were used; sometimes animals were the first block to be seen and at other times plants were the first block. The displays were randomized so that all participants see the displays in a different order in each block.

Procedure

Participants were informed that on half the trials they would see a display of stimuli all from the same category, whereas on the remaining trials a target picture would appear somewhere in the display. Prior to each block, participants were told to search for a specific type of target (either animals or plants). They were also informed that these two types of trial (present or absent) would appear in random order . . . Participants were instructed to press the '/' key [or] the 'z' key . . . Participants were asked to make their responses as quickly and accurately as possible. Each trial began with the presentation of a central fixation cross displayed for 600 **ms** [milliseconds]. Participants were asked to look at the cross. This was followed for 165 ms by a blank screen. Following the blank screen, the search array appeared . . . Reaction times were recorded.

The procedure section states the sequence of events that the participants experience. A within-participants design is used, as all participants experience all conditions. This procedure section also goes into detail about how the displays appear on the screen. A fixation cross is simply a small cross that appears in the centre of the screen to keep the participants' attention in the middle (so that they do not make eye movements, which take up time). The 'search array' is just the display of plants and animals. Note that they measured 'reaction times' (i.e. how fast the participants hit the key). A trial lasts from seeing the fixation cross to responding to the search array.

Results

All trials (6%) on which incorrect responses were made, were excluded from the main reaction time analysis. Mean correct reaction times were analysed in a . . . analysis of variance. The main effects indicated . . . faster reaction times to animal targets (M = 790 ms) than to plant targets (M = 919 ms).

The results section explains what data was collected and how it was analysed. Excluding incorrect responses from the analysis shows that they used only the responses that the participants did correctly. Incorrect trials constituted six per cent of all trials. **Analysis of variance** (ANOVA) is a statistical test which compares the conditions (e.g. target absent v present displays), looking for differences between them. In this experiment, they found faster reaction times to animal than to plant targets. The average time to detect an animal target was 790 ms compared to 919 ms for a plant target. (They do also analyse the rate of incorrect responses, but this is deleted here for simplicity).

Discussion

In Experiment 1, there was evidence for more efficient search for threatening animals among plants, than search for plants among animals. Overall, participants were faster to detect threatening animals among a background of plants, than vice versa. Moreover, increasing the set size from four to nine items was more detrimental to the detection of plants than to the detection of threatening animals . . . In Experiment 1, the average search rate for threatening animals was only 11 ms per item, whereas the search rate for plants was 28 ms per item. Clearly, the difference in search rate between the two types of stimulus are consistent with the idea of fast, efficient detection of threat, in line with the data and suggestions put forward by Öhman *et al.* (1999) . . . However, [the] effect may have been due to the clear, distinct visual properties of animals (in general) compared to those of plants, rather than to the 'threatening' nature of such stimuli.

The discussion section starts by stating what was found. It was found that participants could detect threatening animals among plants faster and more accurately than plants among animals. 'Search rate' refers to how much more time it takes to spot the target for every extra distractor added. This is less for threatening stimuli than for non-threatening stimuli. This suggests that threatening pictures stand out more than non-threatening pictures. The authors state that the findings do support their prediction made in the introduction. They then discuss how the nature of the pictures used may have affected the findings. It is possible that the animals are just more distinctive than plants, rather than more threatening. It is important for researchers to consider the limitations of their method if they want to be sure that their findings are valid. In the rest of this paper, Tipples *et al.* (2002), go on to do four more experiments to explore possible flaws and limitations.

General discussion

The combined findings of all experiments in this research, offer no support for the suggestion that threatening stimuli (attacking animals) will capture anyone's attention more than pleasant stimuli (pleasant animals). Although we were able to replicate findings described by Öhman *et al.* (1999) indicating rapid search for threatening animals, we also found fast search for non-threatening animals and even fruit under certain conditions . . . Therefore, the hypothesis of a general preferential allocation of attention to threat is either incorrect, or the attentional prerequisites of the search paradigm somehow do not tap this process.

In a paper with more than one experiment, there is a discussion for each experiment and then a general discussion which covers all of the experiments. Here we can see that, over all of the five experiments, the findings do not support the idea that the general population show preferential processing to threat. The authors consider whether their hypothesis, that the general population are 'tuned' in to detecting threat, is wrong or whether the method used here (visual search) is not sufficient to find this out.

References

Bradley, B.P., Mogg, K., White, J., Groom, C. and de Bono, J. (1999) Attentional bias for emotional faces in generalized anxiety disorder, *British Journal of Clinical Psychology*, 38: 267–78.

Darwin, C. (1872) *The Expression of the Emotions in Man and Animals*. New York: D. Appleton.

Mogg, K. and Bradley, B.P. (1998) A cognitive-motivational analysis of anxiety, *Behaviour Research and Therapy*, 36: 809–48.

This is the reference section which gives the details of all the sources of information used. Here we give just three taken from the paper (the paper has 21 references in total). The reference section in this book gives references for all those mentioned in the Tipples *et al.* (2002) paper as presented in this chapter.

Summary of Tipples *et al.* (2002)

Tipples and colleagues (2002) examined how well the general population can detect threat by using a visual search task. This task involved seeing how quickly and accurately people could spot a picture of something threatening (animals) compared to something non-threatening (plants). The results of their first experiment did show that the general population could detect threat rapidly and accurately. They found that participants were: (a) faster and more accurate at detecting threatening pictures (animals) than non-threatening pictures (plants); (b) better at finding animals amongst plants than plants amongst animals; and that (c) increasing the number of distractors affected how well they could spot plants, but did not affect how well they could spot animals. These findings suggest that we are better at detecting the threat as it stands out to us more.

However, Tipples *et al.* (2002) questioned whether these findings were due to the nature of the pictures; perhaps the animal pictures were just more distinctive rather than more threatening? So, in the next four experiments, they modified the pictures and method. For example, in Experiment 2 they used plants and pleasant (i.e. non-threatening) animals. The overall results from all five experiments contradicted the findings of Experiment 1. Overall, the five experiments showed that the general population are not able to detect threat quickly. The findings of Experiment 1 were probably due to the nature of the pictures used. Tipples *et al.* (2002) conclude that the overall result is surprising and that more research is needed. It is not unusual to need to modify the way an investigation is done in order to be sure that the results are reliable. We saw that Tipples *et al.* (2002) queried the findings of their Experiment 1 and explored this in a further four experiments. This shows how testing possible explanations for the findings of one experiment enables our understanding to be refined and shows that one explanation can often be limited. By being rigorous and modifying the investigation, we can then be surer that the findings are reliable. If Tipples *et al.* (2002) did not do this, we would have mistakenly accepted Experiment 1's findings.

Summary

You should now have an idea of how psychologists report their research. Looking at one research paper in depth illustrates the format of a paper and the type of information contained in each of its sections. You may also have picked up on some terms related to the method used in the experiment and know more about how humans visually detect threat. This paper should also have given you a feel for the kind of language used in journals. Hopefully, it is not as frightening as it first appears! The next chapter begins Part 2 of this book and our look at the core subject areas in psychology. Your knowledge of the structure of a paper will be useful for these chapters. Chapter 4 focuses on cognitive psychology and looks at one cognitive research paper in depth.

PART 2
The core areas and research papers

We now begin to look at the core areas in psychology (as set out by the BPS). These areas include cognitive psychology, social psychology, developmental psychology, biological psychology and the psychology of individual differences. We also look at the area of clinical psychology.

Each chapter introduces the core area in question and then examines one research paper, in detail, from that area. These research papers are a mixture of recent research papers and older papers, written some time ago by eminent researchers. Some papers investigate new topics and others investigate long-standing issues. The papers use a variety of research methods. The papers are largely as they actually appear in the journals, but some condensing has been done for the sake of simplicity. The purpose of looking at one paper is to give you a flavour of that area and how the research is done. Using just one paper necessitates being very selective from the huge array of research available; it is not possible to include an exhaustive list of research in any area. Nevertheless, you will see that the principles of these research papers are essentially the same.

- Chapter 4, cognitive psychology: do leading questions affect how well we remember an event?
- Chapter 5, social psychology: what factors influence whether a person will help another person in an emergency?
- Chapter 6, developmental psychology: what determines the type of bond a child has with its mother – the child's environment or their genes?
- Chapter 7, biological psychology: does the size of our brains relate to how clever we are?
- Chapter 8, individual differences: does our personality change or stay the same throughout adulthood?
- Chapter 9, clinical psychology: how long do the benefits of cognitive behavioural therapy last for schizophrenia?

4 Cognitive psychology

This chapter describes the area of cognitive psychology and examines one research paper in depth.

- The area: cognitive psychology aims to explain our behaviour by viewing it in terms of what is going on in our minds (our mental processes).
- The research: do leading questions affect how well we remember an event we have seen?

What is cognitive psychology?

Cognitive psychologists are interested in how our mental processes work and how our behaviour relates to how these operate. Cognitive psychology examines how we take in information from the world around us and how we mentally process this information in order to make a response, such as an action or emotion. Cognitive psychology investigates such areas as memory, perception, thinking, language, attention, problem-solving, decision-making and **artificial intelligence**.

Interest in cognitive psychology began to grow during World War Two, when the need to understand how cognitive processes, such as attention, work then became important for applications such as efficient aircraft cockpit design. Behaviourism was the dominant approach in experimental psychology from 1913 to the 1950s, but it was replaced by cognitive psychology in the 1950s. This 'cognitive revolution' occurred as a reaction against behaviourism's sole focus on only observable behaviours. Cognitive psychologists were interested in the processes going on in our minds, which are not directly observable. The beginning of the cognitive revolution is pinpointed to a meeting held in 1956 which featured some of the most influential names in cognitive psychology, such as George Miller and Noam Chomsky. Miller was also partly responsible for founding the Centre for Cognitive Studies at Harvard University in 1960. By the 1970s, the cognitive approach had become the dominant one in psychology. The rise in cognitive psychology was partly related to the development of computer technology; psychologists could make use of its terms in order to talk about the mind. For instance, they could view mental processes in terms of how information was 'input', 'stored' and 'retrieved' and consider the mind as an information processing system which actively organizes and manipulates information.

Research in cognitive psychology studies the mental processes by which we receive information through our senses and make sense of this information (perception), how we store and retrieve information (memory) and how we manipulate that information (thinking). Cognitive psychologists propose that we use such processes to make a mental model of the world around us. This internal, mental model consists of information coming in through our senses and what we already know about how the world works. This existing know-ledge is considered to be represented as schemas. A schema is a network of knowledge about an item (people, actions, objects, abstract concepts) which includes the item's attributes and associations.

As we cannot directly observe the processes going on in our minds, researchers need a way to work out what is going on. To do so, they propose models/theories of how these processes work and, based on these, make predictions about what will happen. For example, researchers can predict what the output will be, based on what information is input and how it is thought to be processed. If the actual output matches what is predicted, then this can be taken as support for the theory/model. Cognitive psychology also takes into account that existing stored knowledge can influence how we interpret incoming information. Cognitive psychology largely uses the research methods of experiments and case studies of brain-damaged individuals. We will next look at a renowned research paper which uses the experimental method to investigate the accuracy of our memory of events.

Research paper

In 1974, Elizabeth Loftus and John Palmer published their findings from two experiments, which examined how the way questions are phrased can affect our memory for an event. Loftus is famous for her research into the fallibility of memory, such as how giving incorrect information after an event can inter-fere with memory and how **false memories** can be triggered in some people just by suggestion. Before we look at Loftus and Palmer's research paper, we will briefly explore the matter of memory.

Background: memory

Memory is fundamental to our lives. Without memory we would have difficulty remembering who we are, what we are meant to be doing and what we have done in the past. We would not be able to recognize people around us, nor would we know how to do things (e.g. our job) or remember facts (e.g. our address).

Memory enables us to process the information coming in through our senses (encoding), store this information (storage) and retrieve it from this store (recall). Problems during any of these stages can result in forgetting. This information processing view considers memory to work both 'backwards' and 'forwards', rather than in one direction from encoding to recall. For instance, information we already hold in memory can influence how we encode new information. Information is held in different memory stores, such as short-term memory (STM), working memory (WM) and long-term memory (LTM). There are also several types of memory. For example, declarative memory holds facts that we can state (declare). Declarative memories fall into two further types: semantic memory and episodic memory. Semantic memory involves our memory for general facts (e.g. meanings, general knowledge), whereas episodic memory is for events and personal experiences linked to a particular time and/or place. In contrast, procedural memory is our knowledge for how we do things (e.g. drive a car).

Information is considered to be stored in LTM as a network of related concepts (a schema), which holds all the information we have related to a unit of information. These schemas affect not only how we interpret and store new information but also how we recall information. Bartlett (1932) argued that people do not just record memories and passively play them back like a tape recorder. Instead, they actively try to make sense of information by fitting it in with what they already know. That is, we 'reconstruct' the information by actively piecing it together using the range of knowledge in the schema. However, reconstructing past information, in light of our schemas, means that we may distort information and our memory may not be entirely correct. For instance, we may be eliminating information that does not fit in with our schema.

Research evidence shows that our memory can indeed be fallible. This inaccuracy has important implications when it comes to such situations, as being an eyewitness of an event and having to recall what you have seen (eyewitness testimony). For example, it is estimated that half, or more, of all wrongful convictions by courts in the United States are partially due to error in what eyewitnesses report that they have witnessed (Huff, 1987). We will now turn to the research paper by Loftus and Palmer (1974) which investigates how information provided after seeing an event ('post-event' information) can affect memory for an event. The paper is presented in segments, each segment being followed by a commentary underneath.

The paper

Loftus, E.F. and Palmer, J.C. (1974) Reconstruction of automobile destruction: an example of the interaction between language and memory, *Journal of Verbal Learning and Verbal Behaviour*, 13: 585–9.

Abstract

Two experiments are reported in which subjects viewed films of auto-mobile accidents and then answered questions about events occurring in the films. The question, 'About how fast were the cars going when they smashed into each other?' elicited higher estimates of speed than ques-tions which used the verbs collided, bumped, contacted, or hit in place of smashed. On a retest one week later, those subjects who received the verb smashed were more likely to say 'yes' to the question, 'Did you see any broken glass?', even though broken glass was not present in the film. These results are consistent with the view that the questions asked subsequent to an event can cause a reconstruction in one's memory of that event.

This is the abstract which summarizes their research. Note that subjects are now called participants.

Introduction

How accurately do we remember the details of a complex event, like a traffic accident, that has happened in our presence? More specifically, how well do we do when asked to estimate some numerical quantity, such as how long the accident took, how fast the cars were travelling, or how much time elapsed between the sounding of a horn and the moment of collision? It is well documented that most people are markedly inaccurate in reporting such numerical details as time, speed, and distance (Bird, 1927; Whipple, 1909) . . . The judgement of speed is especially difficult, and practically every automobile accident results in huge variations from one witness to another, as to how fast a vehicle was actually travelling (Gardner, 1933) . . . In one test administered to Air Force personnel who knew in advance that they would be questioned about the speed of a moving automobile, estimates ranged from 10 to 50 mph (Marshall, 1969, p.23).

Given the inaccuracies in estimates of speed, it seems likely that there are variables which are potentially powerful in terms of influencing these estimates. The present research was conducted to investigate one such variable, namely, the phrasing of the question used to elicit the speed judgement. Some questions are clearly more suggestive than others. This fact of life has resulted in the legal concept of a leading question . . . A leading question is simply one that, either by its form or content, suggests to the witness what answer is desired or leads him to the desired answer. In the present study, subjects were shown films of traffic accidents and then they answered questions about the accident. The subjects were interrogated about the speed of the vehicles in one of several ways. For example, some subjects were asked 'About how fast were the cars going when they hit each other?' while others were asked, 'About how fast were the cars going when they smashed into each other?' As Fillmore (1971), and Bransford and McCarrell (in press [1974]) have noted, *hit* and *smashed* may involve specification of differential rates of movement. Furthermore, the two verbs may also involve differential specification of the likely consequences of the events to which they are referring. The impact of the accident is apparently gentler for *hit* than for *smashed*.

The authors first state the basic research question: how accurately do we remember the details of an event (e.g. a traffic accident)? They base this investigation on previous research which suggests that memory is inaccurate. They then lead into what this research is examining more specifically. They introduce the idea that other factors, such as the phrasing of questions, may affect how well (how accurately) we estimate speed. Leading questions are ones which imply something that may not have happened or been there (e.g. 'Did you see *the* man?' suggests that a man was present even though there may not have been).

They then describe the procedure of this research in more detail. Loftus and Palmer alter the phrasing of the question by changing the verb (hit/ smash). Again, they use previous research evidence to justify their use of verbs. They refer to the paper by Bransford and McCarrell as 'in press'. This means that the research is not yet published but will be in the near future (the paper was actually published later in 1974). The previous research indicates that the two verbs lead us to expect different speeds and outcomes, with 'smashed' being faster and having a worse outcome than 'hit'.

Experiment 1: method

Forty-five students participated in groups of various sizes. Seven films were shown, each depicting a traffic accident . . . The length of the film segments ranged from 5 to 30 sec. Following each film, the subjects received a questionnaire asking them first to 'give an account of the accident you have just seen', and then to answer a series of specific questions about the accident. The critical question was the one that interrogated the subject about the speed of the vehicles involved in the collision. Nine subjects were asked, 'About how fast were the cars going when they hit each other?' Equal numbers of the remaining subjects were interrogated with the verbs *smashed, collided, bumped,* and *contacted* in place of *hit* . . . A different ordering of the films was presented to each group of subjects.

The method section here puts all subsections together; it does not show participants, design and so on, separately. All 45 participants saw all seven films. Note that they do not specifically state what the independent variable (IV) and dependent variable (DV) are. The IV is the change of verb and the DV is the estimate of speed. All participants were given a questionnaire which contained the critical question. The critical question was the one that had the different verbs. Participants were split into five groups of nine participants, each group was presented with one of the verbs (smashed, collided, bumped, contacted or hit). This is a between-participants design. The different ordering of films is to prevent order effects.

Results [of experiment 1]

Table 1 presents the mean speed estimates for the various verbs . . . An analysis of variance was performed . . . yielding a significant [effect at] $p < .005$. Some information about the accuracy of subjects' estimates can be obtained from our data . . . One collision took place at 20 mph, one at 30, and two at 40. The mean estimates of speed for these four films were: 37.7, 36.2, 39.7, and 36.1 mph, respectively. In agreement with previous work, people are not very good at judging how fast a vehicle was actually travelling.

Results sections often include tables and graphs. Loftus and Palmer's Table 1 (see Table 4.1 in this chapter) shows the data summarized as means (averages) and shows that verb 'smashed' produced the fastest speed estimate, whereas the verb 'contacted' produced the slowest. The analysis of variance (ANOVA) shows that the difference between the estimates is significant at the probability level of $p<0.005$ (see Chapter 2).

Discussion [for experiment 1]

The results of this experiment indicate that the form of a question (in this case, changes in a single word) can markedly and systematically affect a witness's answer to that question . . . Two interpretations of this finding are possible. First, it is possible that the differential speed estimates results merely from response-bias factors. A subject is uncertain whether to say 30 mph or 40 mph, for example, and the verb *smashed* biases his response towards the higher estimate. A second interpretation is that the question form causes a change in the subject's memory representation of the accident. The verb *smashed* may change a subject's memory such that he 'sees' the accident as being more severe than it actually was. If this was the case, we might expect subjects to 'remember' other details that did not actually occur, but are commensurate with an accident occurring at higher speeds. The second experiment was designed to provide additional insights into the origin of the differential speed estimates.

The authors consider two possible reasons for these results: the verb may help participants to plump one way or the other, or the verb may actually alter their memory of the event (the verb information is interfering with their original memory). As the authors have two possible interpretations, they will do further testing to examine just how much memory for an event has been altered.

Experiment 2: method

One hundred and fifty students participated in this experiment, in groups of various sizes. A film depicting a multiple car accident was shown . . . [then] the subjects received a questionnaire . . . The critical question was the one that interrogated the subject about the speed of the vehicles. Fifty subjects were asked, 'About how fast were the cars going when they smashed into each other?' Fifty subjects were asked, 'About how fast were the cars going when they hit each other?' Fifty subjects were not interrogated about vehicular speed. One week later, the subjects returned and without viewing the film again they answered a series of questions about the accident. The critical question here was, 'Did you see any broken glass?' which the subjects answered by checking 'yes' or 'no'. This question was embedded in a list totalling 10 questions, and it appeared in a random position in the list. There was no broken glass in the accident, but, since broken glass is commensurate with accidents occurring at high speed, we expected that the subjects who had been asked that *smashed* questions might more often say 'yes' to this critical question.

This procedure is similar to that of experiment 1 but with the alteration that just two verbs were used (smashed, hit) plus a control group who had no question about speed. The IV is the verb used. The DV is the answers to the broken glass question. One week later, they followed-up with a critical question to test whether participants 'remembered' other details that did not actually occur. None of the participants actually saw any broken glass, but broken glass might be expected in accidents at high speed as implied by the verb 'smashed'. The question was positioned randomly, in order to control for the effects of being, for example, first/last in the list.

Results [of experiment 2]

The mean estimate of speed for subjects interrogated with *smashed* was 10.46 mph; with *hit* the estimate was 8.00 mph. These means are significantly different t (98) = 2.00, p<.05. Table 2 presents the distribution of 'yes' and 'no' responses for the *smashed*, *hit* and control subjects. An independence chi-square test . . . was significant beyond the .025 level, χ^2 (2) = 7.76. The important result in table 2 is that . . . smashed leads to both more 'yes' responses and to higher speed estimates. The question now arises: Is *smashed* doing anything else besides increasing the estimate of speed? To answer this . . . [it] appears that the verb smashed has other effects besides that of simply increasing the estimate of speed. One possibility will be discussed in the next section.

They found that the speed estimate was higher for 'smashed' than for 'hit'. These estimates were significantly different (as shown by the **t-test** results t (98) = 2.00, p<.05). Their Table 2 is shown in Table 4.2 in this chapter. The **chi-square** test is used here to look for an association between two variables (the verb used and the likelihood of saying yes/no to the glass question).

Discussion

To reiterate, we have first of all provided an additional demonstration . . . that the way a question is asked can enormously influence the answer that is given. In this instance, the question, 'About how fast were the cars going when they smashed into each other?' led to higher estimates of speed than the same question asked with the verb *smashed* replaced by *hit*. Furthermore, this seemingly small change had consequences for how questions are answered a week after the original event occurred . . . we would like to propose that two kinds of information go into one's memory for some complex occurrence. The first is information gleaned during the perception of the original event; the second is external information supplied after the fact. Over time, information from these two sources may be integrated in such a way that we are unable to tell from which source some specific detail is recalled. All we have is one 'memory' . . . we propose that the subject first forms some representation of the accident he has witnessed. The experimenter then . . . supplies a piece of external information, namely, that the cars did indeed smash into each other. When these two pieces of information are integrated, the subject has a memory of an accident that was more severe that in fact it was. Since broken glass is commensurate with a severe accident, the subject is more likely to think that broken glass was present.

The discussion begins by summarizing the findings from the experiments and states that this study does support previous research. This has important implications for how eyewitnesses' accounts can be influenced after the event by subsequent information. (e.g. being questioned by police, discussing the event with others). They propose that our memory of seeing the event combines with the information received post-event to form one memory. In our schema of a car accident, we would expect to see broken glass at an accident. Loftus and Palmer do list all their references, but for brevity the references mentioned in this summary are in the reference section at the end of this book.

Table 4.1 Loftus and Palmer's (1974) Table 1: speed estimates for the verbs used in experiment one

Verb	Mean speed estimate
Smashed	40.8
Collided	39.3
Bumped	38.1
Hit	34.0
Contacted	31.8

Table 4.2 Loftus and Palmer's (1974) Table 2: distribution of 'yes' and 'no' responses to the question 'Did you see any broken glass?'

Response	Verb condition Smashed	Hit	Control
Yes	16	7	6
No	34	43	44

Summary of Loftus and Palmer (1974)

Loftus and Palmer's (1974) experiments show that our memory for an event can be influenced by information we receive after the event. This suggests that an eyewitness testimony (EWT) may contain not only what the person saw but possibly also information obtained later (e.g. which could come from other witnesses, police and so on). As this research involved laboratory experiments, it can be criticized for having low ecological validity. However, doing research in a laboratory means that it can effectively control unwanted variables. Loftus and colleagues have conducted many follow-up studies to examine this issue further.

Research into EWT shows how cognitive psychology research can be applied to the real world. Such research has developed ways to improve the reliability of EWT. For instance, psychologists can be 'expert witnesses' who go into court to explain to the jury that EWT may be unreliable and inaccurate. Furthermore, psychologists have developed the cognitive interview (CI), which is a way of interviewing eyewitnesses that helps them to recall more information and more accurately (e.g. Geiselman, Fisher, MacKinnon and Holland, 1985). A CI uses techniques to enhance memory, reduce the number of interruptions and stop the use of leading questions, when an eyewitness recalls the event to an interviewer (e.g. policeman). For example, the eyewitness mentally recreates the context they were in (context reinstatement), reports everything he/she can think of about the event (free recall), reports details in different orders (change order) and reports events from a different perspective (change perspective). Geiselman and colleagues found that recall was better and more accurate with the cognitive interview compared to the standard police interview. Box 4.1 gives two summaries of other research in cognitive psychology.

Summary of cognitive psychology

Research in cognitive psychology has been used in such matters as improving eyewitness testimony, improving attention and providing therapies (e.g. therapies for depression which concentrate on disordered thoughts). Critics of the cognitive psychology approach consider it to have an overly simplistic view of behaviour and to largely lack ecological validity as it uses laboratories and experimental methods. However, this does allow for a control over unwanted factors. Although the cognitive approach has also been criticized for ignoring social and emotional factors, it has become increasingly integrated with, and influenced by, other approaches to form such fields as social cognition and cognitive neuropsychology. For example, cognitive neuropsychology integrates cognitive psychology with neuropsychology, looking at how mental processes operate normally and when impaired in brain-damaged patients. The next chapter examines an area, social psychology, which focuses more on the external factors affecting our behaviour than the internal mental processes as in cognitive psychology.

 Box 4.1 Research: other research in cognitive psychology

There has been much ongoing research into eyewitness testimony. These two summaries of more recent studies illustrate how research progresses in a particular topic.

Wise and Safer (2004): Judges' beliefs about eyewitness testimony
Wise and Safer (2004) conducted a survey (using questionnaires) to examine what judges in the United States know and believe about eyewitness testimony. This is an important issue as unreliable eyewitness testimony can lead to wrongful convictions. They questioned 160 judges to examine: their knowledge about factors affecting eyewitness reliability; their beliefs about juror's knowledge of factors affecting eyewitnesses (e.g. whether eyewitness confidence is a good indication of their accuracy); and their willingness to allow lawyers to use safeguards (e.g. expert witnesses). They found that judges had limited understanding, such as being unfamiliar with studies showing that over half of all wrongful convictions are due to eyewitness error. However, they did find that increased knowledge about eyewitness testimony related to such factors as judges being more willing to use expert witnesses and being more reluctant to convict a person based solely on eyewitness testimony.

Holliday and Albon (2004): Using the cognitive interview with young children
Holliday and Albon examined whether variations of the cognitive interview (CI) improved young children's recall of an event and reduced their suggestibility to misinformation. It had been found previously that a child's recall can be distorted by being questioned often by police, social workers, lawyers, and so on (Ceci and Bruck, 1995). In Holliday and Albon's investigation, young children (4- to 5-year-olds) watched a five-minute video of a birthday party. The next day a researcher talked to each child and gave them some misinformation. A second researcher then interviewed the child using different versions of a CI. For example, one version contained free recall, context reinstatement and change order, but not change perspective. They found that a short CI was more efficient with young children. Recall was more accurate when using the free recall, context reinstatement and change order parts of the CI. Children were less suggestible to misinformation when the CI used free recall and context reinstatement.

5 Social psychology

This chapter describes what social psychology encompasses and then examines one research paper in detail.

- The area: social psychology views our behaviour in its social context.
- The research: what factors influence whether a person will help another person in an emergency?

What is social psychology?

Other people affect our behaviour, and we affect theirs, in many ways. Social psychology examines how people affect each other, both as individuals and as groups, and how the society they form influences people's behaviour, thoughts and emotions. For example, in certain situations we may conform to the people around us so as to not appear ill-informed or we may show aggression to people outside of our own group (e.g. to fans of an opposing football team). Social psychology includes several fields. The field of social influence is concerned with how we influence others and how they influence us (e.g. studying conformity or leadership). Social development focuses on how we develop over time as a result of society's expectations, our changing roles in society and cultural influences. Social cognition refers to how we think about others and ourselves (e.g. attitudes, stereotyping). Social behaviour refers to how we behave in dyads (two-person groups) and groups (e.g. studying attraction or helping behaviour).

Social psychology developed in the late eighteenth/early nineteenth century, from such areas as the German *Völkerpsychologie* which studied the social nature of the mind, and from such work as Le Bon's examination of the laws of how people behave when they form a crowd. His book (*The Crowd*, 1896) is considered to mark the beginning of modern social psychology. Norman Triplett (1898) is generally attributed with conducting the 'first' social psychology experiment which examined how the mere presence of other people in a task, boosted performance (**social facilitation**). The development of social psychology in America and Europe differed in the emphasis placed on the behaviour of individuals in society, compared with how society operates in a larger role. Social psychology has been a distinct subject area in Britain since the Second World War and is now firmly established.

Social psychology research uses a wide range of research methods, including field research, observations, laboratory experiments and surveys (questionnaires and interviews). We will now turn to one research paper which uses an experimental method, along with observation and questionnaires, to investigate people's helping behaviour.

Research paper

Fischer, Greitemeyer, Pollozek and Frey published their findings from an experiment into how bystanders behave in 2006. Before we look at their research paper in detail, we will briefly review the topic of bystander behaviour.

Background: pro-social behaviour and the bystander effect

Pro-social behaviour is behaviour which benefits others, such as when a bystander helps someone. Much research has been conducted to investigate which factors determine whether a bystander will help another person or not. This research was largely instigated by the famous case of Kitty Genovese's murder.

Kitty Genovese, a 28-year-old woman, was repeatedly stabbed over a half-hour period when she was going home in the early morning of 13 March, 1964. Thirty-eight witnesses heard her screams, and some watched from their windows, but only one witness called the police. This event led two psychologists, Latané and Darley, to investigate what factors determine if people will help or not. For example, in one study Darley and Latané (1968) had participants in individual rooms, discussing personal problems with others via microphones and headphones. The participants were led to believe that one, two, three or six other people were present but in reality there were no other people (they actually heard tape recordings). They were also led to believe that one of these people was prone to seizures. They then overheard a person having a seizure. It was found that 100 per cent of the participants went for help when they thought that they were the only person to know. However, when the participants thought that there were more people to help, they went for help less often. The research suggested that the more bystanders there are, the less help will be given; this became known as the bystander effect.

Further research has determined that both features of the situation, and personal factors, influence whether a bystander will offer help (e.g. the number of other bystanders present, the person's similarity to the victim). In addition, other research indicates that the characteristics of the victim influence whether help is offered. For example, Piliavin *et al.* (1969) conducted a field experiment (see Table 2.3) where a male confederate collapsed and remained on the floor until he received help (a confederate helped after 70 seconds if no one else did). They found that victims that appeared to be ill were more likely to receive help (100 per cent help) and receive it more quickly than victims who seemed to be drunk (81 per cent help). Men were significantly more likely to help than women and there was a tendency for same race helping.

One explanation for bystander behaviour is the arousal:cost-reward model, proposed by Dovidio *et al.* (1991). This model proposes that bystanders decide whether to help based on (a) the arousal they experience due to witnessing someone in distress and (b) their analysis of the costs and rewards for helping (or not helping). Costs include, for example, possible physical harm if they help or guilt if they do not. Rewards include, for example, praise from victim if they help or being able to go about their own business as normal, if they do not help. This model is considered in the research paper by Fischer *et al.* (2006).

The paper

Fischer, P., Greitemeyer, T., Pollozek, F. and Frey, D. (2006) The unresponsive bystander: are bystanders more responsive in dangerous emergencies? *European Journal of Social Psychology*, 36: 267–78.

Abstract

Previous research in bystander intervention found that the presence of other bystanders reduces helping behaviour in an emergency (bystander effect). The research was mainly conducted in the context of non-dangerous, non-violent emergencies. We hypothesize that the classic bystander effect does not occur in more dangerous situations because: a) they are faster and more clearly recognized as emergency situations; and b) higher costs for refusing help increase the accepted costs for helping. Following this line of reasoning, the present research tests whether the bystander effect is affected by the degree of the emergency's potential danger. Results supported our expectations. In situations with low potential danger, more help was given in the solitary condition, than in the bystander condition. However, in situations with high potential danger, participants confronted with an emergency alone, or in the presence of another bystander, were similarly likely to help the victim.

This is the abstract which summarizes the aims and findings of the research.

Introduction

Much publicity has been given in recent years to those incidents, in which crimes are committed, while bystanders do nothing to help the victim – such as the widely decried unresponsiveness of 38 witnesses during the violent murder of Kitty Genovese. However, there are also examples to prove the opposite, such as the incident that happened in Munich . . . 2001 . . . Some Nazi skinheads chased a young Greek and beat him up in a most brutal way. Several people witnessed this situation and one of them – a young man from Turkey – decided to help. Risking his own life, he was able to save the bloodstained victim's life. With regard to these examples, the following question arises: What is the difference between emergencies in which bystanders do help and those in which bystanders do not help? In our opinion, the subjectively perceived danger of the emergency plays an important role in this context. However, the role of emergency-related danger for the bystander intervention, has not been fully investigated thus far. Accordingly, in the current study we mainly investigate whether different degrees of emergency-related danger differently affect helping responses of bystanders, who are either alone or in the company of another passive bystander. In order to further clarify underlying psychological processes, we try to investigate associations between emergency-related danger, bystander presence, emergency awareness and accepted costs of intervention.

This part of the introduction shows how research can be prompted by, and be relevant to, questions arising from real-life incidents. As the bystander behaviour in the cases of Kitty Genovese and the young Greek man is contradictory, the question arises as to what determines the difference in behaviour in these situations. The researchers introduce the factor (perceived level of danger) which they consider to determine bystanders' helping behaviour. They also state that this has not yet been fully examined in previous research, which is why this piece of research is needed. They will examine how a person responds when there are (a) different levels of danger and (b) when they are alone or with another person (bystander). The bystander is said to be passive as they will not be initiating any help.

Research on bystander intervention

Research on bystander intervention (Latané and Darley, 1970) provided strong support for the general proposition that the presence of other people serves to inhibit the impulse to help. Furthermore, the mere perception that other people are also witnessing the event will markedly decrease the likelihood that an individual will intervene in an emergency (Darley and Latané, 1968; Latané and Rodin, 1969). Latané and Darley (1970) have proposed three different processes that may account for the frequently observed tendency of bystanders to inhibit each other's responsiveness in emergencies: a) social influence; b) evaluation apprehension; and c) diffusion of responsibility ... The bystander effect has been replicated in a variety of experimental situations (**cf** Latané and Nida, 1981). For example, when a room with people waiting for an interview became filled with smoke (Latané and Darley, 1968) ... [or] when other persons suffered a seizure (Schwartz and Clausen, 1970) ... All of these studies have found social inhibition effects, that is, bystanders hinder helping behaviour ... yet little of this research has confronted subjects with an emergency caused by a violent crime with potentially severe and dangerous negative consequences, both for the bystander and the victim (e.g. getting ... attacked by the perpetrator) ... In most research conducted to date, bystanders have been exposed to violent situations with only little potential danger and few potential negative consequences for bystanders and victims, such as in the form of fighting between children (Latané and Darley, 1970) ... In none of these studies were the victims or the bystanders in real danger, such as being hit or insulted by a perpetrator.

This section of the introduction refers to previous research which shows that helping behaviour is affected by the presence of other people (bystanders) or even just believing that other bystanders are present. The presence of other bystanders results in people being less likely to help. Social influence includes when, in an unclear situation, people will look to others' responses to see how to interpret the situation (so if other people do not help, you may not help either). Evaluation apprehension, refers to the fear of being negatively judged by others. Diffusion of responsibility is when we can share the responsibility to help with other people present and so be less responsible individually. The researchers state that previous research is limited, as there has not been much danger potentially for the bystander or victim (which can happen in real life).

Bystander intervention in dangerous emergencies

There are only a few studies investigating the bystander effect by exposing participants to a dangerous, violent emergency (Harari *et al.*, 1985;

Schwartz and Gottlieb, 1976) implying high costs for helping (danger for the bystander) but also high costs for not helping (danger for the victim). For example . . . [in] Harari *et al.* (1985) . . . a rape situation was simulated in a naturalistic setting. In sum . . . [when] participants were confronted with dangerous emergencies [they] more frequently helped in the bystander conditions than in the alone conditions. Hence, violent and dangerous emergencies seem to reduce the bystander effect. However, since none of these studies employed a control group with low potential danger to a bystander and victim, we cannot definitely conclude that the perceived danger of the emergency is a crucial moderator for the occurrence of a bystander effect. The present study tries to overcome this flaw of former research on bystander intervention.

Why do dangerous emergencies seemingly reduce the bystander effect? We assume that dangerous emergencies are recognized as real emergencies more clearly and thus increase the costs for not helping the victim. As a consequence, the bystander's **empathic** arousal increases, which finally leads to more helping – independently of whether the bystander is alone or accompanied by other bystanders . . . In the context of dangerous emergences (i.e. when the costs for not helping are high either to the bystander or the victim) this model would predict a generally increased empathic arousal, and thus – independently of whether the bystander is alone or not – increased helping rates. The present study intends to directly test this hypothesis.

In this part of the introduction, they show that some studies have been conducted with high potential danger. These studies found that higher danger reduced the bystander effect (i.e. the presence of others did not affect help being offered). However, a problem with these studies is that they did not use a control condition; they only used high potential danger (see Chapter 2 and glossary). Again, this is why this research is important.

Empathic arousal is the arousal experienced from empathizing with a person in distress (taking the perspective of someone in need). These studies used an 'alone' condition, where the participant witnessed the event alone, and a 'bystander' condition, where the participant witnessed the event in the company of other people. Their hypothesis is that increased danger increases empathic arousal, which increases helping behaviour regardless of whether a bystander is present or not. As well as examining the effect of degree of danger and presence of bystander, Fischer *et al.* (2006) examine the components of the arousal:cost-reward model. For the purposes of simplicity in this chapter, their examination and discussion of this model will not be included here.

The present study
Participants were exposed to an emergency situation, with either low or high potential danger to the victim and the bystander. In it, the bystander was either alone or in the presence of one additional passive bystander, a confederate of the experimenter who had been instructed to notice the emergency but to remain indifferent to it. The participant's alleged task was to evaluate a cross-gender communication between a man and a woman. Suddenly, the man starts to verbally attack and grab the woman. The degree of potential emergency-related danger was manipulated by the size of the male actor who was either of small stature (representing low danger) or of large stature (representing high danger). In accordance with the arousal:cost-reward model, we hypothesize that the classic bystander effect will be replicated in conditions with low but not in those with high danger . . . Note that this study is the first one comparing intervention frequency in emergency situations with low and high expected danger for the helper and the potential victim; previous studies did not systematically manipulate this variable within the same experimental design. . . .

In this study, the victim is a person who is involved in acting out an emergency scenario. The 'bystander' is the true participant. In one condition, there is another bystander who is actually a confederate (i.e. a person who is 'in' on the experiment, in contrast to the participant who does not know the real purpose of the experiment).

Method

Participants and design
Participants were 54 females and 32 males, between the ages of 18 and 34 years old (M = 23.70, SD = 3.59) who received 5 Euro (about $6.50) for participation. A 2 (*bystander:* yes *v* no) × 2 (*danger:* low *v* high) × 2 (*sex of bystander:* female *v* male) . . . design was employed. All participants were randomly assigned to the experimental conditions. The entire experiment lasted for about 1 h [hour].

M is the mean (average) age; SD is the standard deviation of the ages, which is how much the ages vary around the average age. This shows the independent variables (IVs) used in this research. Each IV has two levels. For instance, the bystander IV has the levels of there being no other bystander present (no: where the participant is alone) and of there being another bystander (yes: where the confederate is present).

Materials and procedure

A hallway in the university building was the designated meeting point for all participants. The participants learned that their task was to evaluate a cross-gender communication. Written instructions indicated that the study tested the hypothesis that in a first contact situation, between men and women, the judgement of the actual sexual interest of the opposite sex is frequently subject to misinterpretation . . . Each participant was collected by the experimenter and accompanied to the participants' room. To ensure that the participants knew the location of the experimenter's office, the experimenter stopped briefly at his office to get some questionnaires while the participant waited at the door. Then, the target room in which the cross-gender communication was to take place was shown to the participants to ensure that they knew its location and to make them familiar with the technical equipment involved in the experiment . . . participants were led next door to their room, which was equipped with a TV in front of a table and two chairs for them to watch and evaluate the social interaction sequence.

In the participants' room, the participants were given written instructions together with the social interaction questionnaire. Participants learned that they would secretly observe three interactions between different randomly chosen pairs of subjects who did not know each other. The camera in the target room would transmit the cross-gender interaction live onto the TV screen in the participants' room. The participants were supposed to observe the three subsequent interactions between the two opposite sex individuals and to thoroughly evaluate the interaction afterwards. The questionnaire involved 11 items measuring how attracted the individuals were to each other (e.g. 'Do you think they will meet each other again after the experiment?'). These data were not analysed. After having read the instructions, the subject was left alone and the experiment began by randomly showing the videotape either with low or high potentially negative consequences in the third interaction sequence.

Written instructions are used so that they will be exactly the same for all participants. This is important for controlling for unwanted variables (e.g. if the researchers spoke the instructions, they may differ slightly each time, which may affect the participants' responses or expectations). Likewise, all stages of the procedure (e.g. stopping by the office) were done in exactly the same way for all participants. Participants were misled about the real purpose of the experiment so that their 'true' behaviour could be recorded. They believed that the study tested how men and women judge the sexual interest of the opposite sex, whereas it was actually testing helping behaviour. Participants were shown both rooms so that they would know where to go in order to intervene in the attack or to get help. In the target room, there was a video camera which the participants believed would be transmitting a live signal, but they actually saw previously taped interactions. The social interaction questionnaire leads the participants to believe that they are judging the sexual interest of the men and women. The data from these questionnaires is not used as it is not for the real purpose of the research. The video shows three interactions; the third interaction is the one that shows the attack.

> *Manipulation of the potential danger of the emergency*
> The experimental stimuli consisted of two pre-recorded videos each showing three interaction sequences between three different males and three different females. The first two interaction sequences were exactly identical on both videotapes . . . In the third sequence, professional actors were recruited. The female actor representing the victim in both third sequences was a 21-year-old petite female, with a fragile physique. Her counterpart on the video sequence with *high potential danger* was a strong-built, thug-like male . . . The actors were pre-instructed to become acquainted and flirt . . . the male actor was instructed to increase sexual insinuation up to a level of unambiguous verbal sexual harassment . . . In the fifth minute, the male perpetrator loudly starts insulting the victim and touching her without permission. The conflict peaks in the victim's attempts to stand up and prepare to leave the room, while the perpetrator tries to block the exit. While the victim screams . . . the perpetrator pushes her roughly across the room into the far end corner. A few seconds later the picture goes black leaving the watching participant with this last impression of the emergency. The same actress's counterpart on the second video sequence with low potential danger was a skinny male of small stature, eliciting much less fear and respect . . . The course of this sequence was completely identical to the sequence with high potentially negative consequences. Both videos were pilot tested.

There are two videos; one with the low danger scenario and one with the high danger scenario. Again, unwanted extraneous variables are controlled for by keeping the first two interaction sequences the same, only the third differs in terms of danger. Pilot testing is when materials and/or the procedure are tested on a small sample of people before doing the research. This is done here to ensure that the videos do have the intended effect (i.e. that they do portray low and high danger). They asked people to watch the videos and assess, for example, how dangerous the situation is for the victim and for the bystander to intervene. They found that the high danger sequence actually was felt to be more dangerous to the victim and bystander, than the low danger one.

Manipulation of the bystander v no-bystander condition

In the no-bystander condition, the participant was alone in the participants' room . . . In the bystander condition, the participant watched the video sequences in the presence of a bystander who was a confederate . . . During the third critical sequence, the bystander would watch the incident apathetically and answer the questionnaire subsequently. If the bystander was approached by the participant, he/she would acknowledge the incident with a quick notion, shrug shoulders, and continue to exhibit no signs of upset. If again addressed by the participant, the bystander would only respond that s/he does not want to get involved, his/her job is answering the questionnaire.

Dependent measures

The experimenter observed from a hidden location and checked whether the participant tried to help the victim. Before the participant could enter the target room, he/she was stopped by the experimenter and assured that everything was under control. In addition, the experimenter measured reaction times of the participants from the end of the third sequence (when the screen went black) until they left the lab in order to help the victim. Of course, this data could only be measured for participants who intervened. Finally, all participants were asked to answer one more questionnaire that contained items measuring social responsibility, accepted costs for intervention, and awareness that an emergency really happened . . . Participants were given the suspicion check asking whether they perceived the three interaction sequences as real and authentic, and if they believed that the observed pair was actually physically present in the target room. Finally, participants were thoroughly debriefed.

Dependent measures are the same as dependent variables (see Chapter 2 and glossary). The dependent variables (DVs) are (a) whether the participant intervened (trying to help the victim), (b) reaction times (how long they took to intervene) and (c) a questionnaire that measured aspects of the arousal:cost-reward model. Social responsibility was measured with, for example, 'I felt personally responsible for helping in that emergency situation'. In this chapter, we will focus on the first two DVs only. The suspicion check is to ensure that participants really did believe what they were seeing. Debriefing is particularly important when deception is used.

Results

Thirty-seven per cent of the participants tried to help the victim. Sex and age of the participants and sex of the bystander, had no effect on any of the dependent variables . . . Thus, these variables are not considered further here.

Suspicion check

Two persons were excluded from the sample prior to analysis because they did not believe that the social interaction sequences were really happening next door.

Helping behaviour

Less intervention occurred in the condition with low potential danger (31.7%) than in the condition with high potential danger (41.9%) . . . Follow-up analyses revealed a significant interaction between bystander and response in the condition with low danger . . . Whereas 50% of the participants tried to help the victim when they were alone, only 5.9% tried to help the victim when a bystander was present. In contrast, the interaction between bystander and response was not significant in the condition with high potential danger . . . Whereas 44.4% of the partici- pants tried to help the victim when they were alone, 40% tried to help when a bystander was present. That is, the classic bystander effect was replicated when the situation involved low potential danger but not when the situation involved high potential danger.

Reaction time

A 2 (danger) $\times$ 2 (bystander) ANOVA with reaction time in seconds as a dependent variable, revealed a marginal significant main effect of danger . . . indicating that participants in the high danger condition . . . reacted faster than participants in the low danger condition.

This is an abridged version of the results, as we are not considering Fischer *et al.*'s (2006) examination of the arousal:cost-reward model here. They found that people offered less help when there was low danger, than when there was high danger. The presence of a bystander did affect people's helping response when there was low danger, but it did not affect helping response when there was high danger. 'Interaction' means that the two factors, of whether a bystander was present and the amount of danger, act on each other. It is significant, which means that this finding would not be expected to have occurred by chance. 'Not significant' means that there is no real difference between 44.4% and 40% – so there is no difference in behaviour when there is high danger. The time it took for participants to intervene (reaction times) was analysed, using analysis of variance (ANOVA). They found that people reacted faster when there was high danger.

Discussion

Whereas previous research in the context of low dangerous emergencies has shown that bystanders systematically reduce the frequency of helping (bystander effect), the present study revealed that in the context of highly dangerous emergencies, this bystander effect does not occur ... the present study is the first to systematically compare bystander inter-vention, with one or two bystanders, in the context of low and high dangerous emergencies. Since former studies mainly used either only low ... or only high ... dangerous emergency situations, the present study provides valuable new insights concerning this context. In addi-tion, the present study might alter the still negative perspective and implications surrounding the bystander effect thus far. The probability of receiving help decreases with an increasing number of bystanders. How-ever, with regard to our research, this effect is restricted to non-dangerous emergencies. When people are in real trouble, they have a good chance to receive help even when more than one bystander is present in the emergency situation.

Limitations and directions for future research
First, we have to question whether participants really believed that the emergency situation was real. However, only two participants reported doubts as to the reality of the scenario. Moreover, observations of the experimenter and the confederate confirmed the plausibility of the experimental procedure, as most participants were clearly in a state of emotional distress when watching the victim's need. Second, in our study, danger to the bystander is **confounded** with danger to the victim (as well as others in this vein and many real life emergencies). Therefore, we cannot distinguish whether our effects were due to increased danger to the bystander, increased danger to the victim, or both. It would be a fruitful endeavour for future research to manipulate both independently from one another ...

Third, and finally, although the present study measured helping responses and reaction times, further behavioural data could have been provided in order to investigate our hypothesis. For example, additional observations could have been made, such as: a) did those who inter-vened first initiate a conversation with the bystander at an early rather than a late point in time ... d) did they conspicuously avoid eye contact with the confederate?

The researchers conclude that they have found that, in high danger, people offer help even when in the presence of others. That is, the bystander effect does not happen in high danger scenarios. An important part of research is recognizing its limitations and considering modifications. The researchers address this here by discussing the suspicion check and so on.

Summary of Fischer *et al.* (2006)

This research shows that the context people are in, determines whether the bystander effect occurs. When people perceive a high danger situation, the presence of other people does not affect their helping behaviour. Fischer *et al.*'s findings support the arousal:cost-reward model. They suggest that danger is recognized faster and more clearly as being an emergency situation when other bystanders are present. Also, in the high danger situation, participants are more ready to accept the costs of helping than in the low danger situation, as the costs of not helping are higher when there is high danger. Their study shows how research is relevant to the real world. Some summaries of other recent research in this area are given in Box 5.1.

Summary of social psychology

Social psychology takes into account the fact that we live as social beings. It explains many phenomena and has a wide range of practical applications, such as health issues and criminal behaviour. For example, we can use what we know from research about persuasion to encourage people to give up smoking, or use research evidence to help reduce **labelling** in educational settings. Social psychology provides evidence from a wide range of research methods. This approach is, however, criticized for underestimating the individual differences which people may bring to a social situation.

 Box 5.1 Research: other research in social psychology

Garcia, Weaver, Moskowitz and Darley (2002): Thinking about groups of other people
Garcia *et al.* (2002) examined whether just thinking about being in a group could lead to the bystander effect occurring. In their study, they 'primed' participants with the idea of being in a group by asking them, for instance, to 'Imagine you won a dinner for yourself and 30 of your friends at your favourite restaurant' or 'Imagine that you and a friend are sitting in a crowded movie theatre.' They varied the imagined group size so that the participants imagined 30 other people, ten other people or one other person. They also used a neutral condition (where participants did not imagine any group). The priming is intended to

trigger the concepts and knowledge associated with being in a group. Garcia *et al.* then asked participants to state how much of their annual earnings they would give to charity. They found that the participants thinking about groups of 30 other people would give less to charity than those thinking about ten other people, one other person and the neutral condition. They found this effect even when people imagined being in groups which would not be of any help in the future situation (i.e. being in a movie theatre with strangers would not relate to giving to a University alumni fund). This research adds to previous research by showing that the bystander effect does not just occur when people are actually in a group of bystanders, or think they are in presence of others, but also when they just think about groups.

Chekroun and Brauer (2002): Social control and the bystander effect
Chekroun and Brauer (2002) examined whether the presence of bystanders would affect people's use of social control with someone they perceived to be behaving badly. In any group, there are unstated rules for what behaviours are acceptable, which are called social norms. When people break these norms, their behaviour is considered to be deviant. Group members may communicate their disapproval of deviant behaviour (e.g. by tutting), which is called social control. Chekroun and Brauer (2002) tested whether people are less likely to exert social control when in the presence of bystanders using two situations: where there was low and high personal implication for the person witnessing the deviant behaviour. In the low implication situation, participants saw a person drawing graffiti in a shopping centre lift (this is considered to have low implication as the lift belongs to a corporation). In the high implication situation, participants witnessed litter being dropped in a park (this is considered to have high implication as the park's maintenance is paid for by the taxes of local residents). They predicted that the bystander effect will not occur in the park situation (high implication) but will in the lift situation (low implication). In both situations, they used confederates who carried out the deviant behaviour and then observed and recorded the bystanders' responses. It was found that the bystander effect did occur in the low implication setting (the lift) but did not occur in high implication setting (the park). Chekroun and Brauer (2002) conclude that this shows that personal implication is an important factor in bystander behaviour.

6 Developmental psychology

In this chapter, we examine the area of developmental psychology and one developmental research paper in detail.

- The area: developmental psychology studies our behaviour at different ages and how our behaviour changes over time.
- The research: what determines the type of bond a child has with its mother – the child's environment or their **genes?**

What is developmental psychology?

Developmental psychology considers how we develop over our lifespan, from conception to old age. It is concerned with how behaviours change, or stay constant, as we get older. These behaviours include, for example, our cognitive, moral, **motor**, social, and personality development. Developmental psychology is also interested in the stages in our lifetime, such as infancy, adolescence and middle adulthood.

Historically, interest in development focused on whether we are born with a clean slate, on which experience works to make us what we are as adults, or whether our adult abilities and personality are predetermined at birth. For example, John Locke (1634–1704) saw the human mind as a *tabula rasa* (blank slate) which was influenced by experience during development. Many intellectuals have observed and noted how children develop, such as Charles Darwin (1877), who recorded his own son's development of fear, affection and so on. Milicent Shinn recorded the first complete observation of a child's development. She kept daily notes from observing her niece and published these in *The Biography of a Baby* in 1900. Regarding intellectual development, two leading developmentalists, Piaget (1896–1980) and Vygotsky (1896–1934), respectively suggested that children go through a set of predetermined stages of intellectual development, or that the human environment shapes intellectual development via social interaction. Although the area of developmental psychology initially focused on child development, it has extended to incorporate changes in people across the whole lifespan.

Developmental psychology uses a diverse range of research methods, including experiments, observations, surveys, cross-sectional studies, longitudinal studies and twin studies. For example, interviews can be used to examine people's adjustment to retirement, whereas longitudinal studies can be used to see how children's reading skill develops over time. The research paper, examined in this chapter, uses an observational method in a twin study to investigate how one aspect of our social behaviour changes as we develop.

Research paper

The research by Caroline Bokhorst and colleagues, examines the type of emotional bond that develops between an infant and its primary caregiver (e.g. mother, father). It specifically examines how much a child's environment and their genes affect the type of bond they show. Before we look at their research in detail, we will review what this bond is, as well as how we can examine how much genetics and environment affect people's behaviour.

Background: attachment, genes and environments

Psychologists refer to a strong and long-lasting emotional bond between two people as an attachment. Attachments can form across the entire lifespan, but the first of human attachments is between the infant and its primary caregiver. The primary caregiver can be the mother, father, a grandparent and so on, but the mother-child attachment is the most commonly discussed (from here on, we will refer to the mother for simplicity). Attachment generally begins between 6 and 8 months old, when babies start to distinguish who their own mother is. The type of attachment shown differs between individuals. Mary Ainsworth and colleagues, developed a way of classifying these different types of attachment using the Strange Situation (see Box 6.1).

People not only vary in their type of attachments but also in many other **traits** and behaviours, such as their response to stress, how intelligent they are, susceptibility to mental illness or weight gain. These differences between individuals arise from the influences we receive from two sources: one source is the environment we develop and live in (e.g. parents, nutrition) and the other is biological factors (i.e. our genes). Biological influences are often referred to as 'nature' and environmental factors as 'nurture'. Note that it is not the case of nature *versus* nurture, so much as an interaction between both factors that influences how we develop. This is known as gene/environment interaction.

Box 6.1 Methods: the Strange Situation procedure

Ainsworth, Blehar, Waters and Wall (1978) developed the Strange Situation procedure to examine how individuals differ in their attachment. The Strange Situation involves a laboratory observation where the child is separated from, and reunited with, their primary caregiver (usually the mother). The infant's reaction to separation from the mother is used to assess and classify attachment 'styles'. It focuses on the way the child balances attachment and exploring behaviours when under moderate stress due to being separated. Generally, the procedure involves the mother and child being taken to an unfamiliar room and experiencing a set of scenarios in seven, three-minute episodes. For example:

1   Mother and child enter a room which has toys in it. The child can explore and play while the mother is present.
2   A stranger joins the mother and child.
3   The mother leaves the child with the stranger.
4   The mother returns and resettles the child, the stranger leaves.
5   The mother leaves and the child is alone.
6   The stranger enters and interacts with the lone child.
7   The mother returns again and the stranger leaves.

Ainsworth *et al.* (1978) identified three main types of attachment (also called classifications, patterns, categories or groups) for children up to 20 months old. These are:

1   *Type B, secure attachment*
    The child plays happily using the mother as a base for exploration. Child is distressed by mother leaving. When reunited, the child shows positive gestures/smiles, and tries to get close to and/or interact with the mother. This child is not opposed to stranger contact but treats strangers differently from mother.
2   *Type A, insecure attachment-avoidant/detached*
    The child shows little secure behaviour. The child ignores the mother and is not affected by her leaving or returning, child actively avoids and ignores mother when reunited. Although the child is distressed when alone, he/she is easily comforted by strangers.
3   *Type C, insecure attachment-ambivalent (resistant)*
    The child is fretful or passive while with mother. The child is distressed when she leaves, but angry with the mother on reunion or not easily soothed by the mother. The child may resist contact with the mother and stranger.
       Ainsworth *et al.*'s types are considered as organized types. Main and Solomon (1986) identified a fourth category, which is a disorganized type:

4   *Type D, insecure attachment – disorganized (disoriented)*
The child does not show a predictable attachment response, but displays a diverse array of behaviours in response to the stranger and the stress of the procedure.

- Note that the term 'insecure' is sometimes called 'anxious'.
- Ainsworth *et al.* (1978) found that, for American infants (12 to 18 months old), 70 per cent were securely attached, 20 per cent were avoidant and 10 per cent, ambivalent.
- Van Ijzendoorn and Kroonenberg (1988) found that secure attachments are also the most common type in other cultures, but there is a higher rate of insecure-avoidant attachment in Western Europe and of insecure-ambivalent attachment in Israel and Japan.
- Research suggests that what this early attachment is like, can have some consequences for the quality of future relationships (although other factors also affect future attachments). For example, Grossmann and Grossmann (1991) found that a child securely attached to its mother as a baby, is more likely to enjoy close friendships later in childhood.
- These attachment patterns seem to be relatively stable over time. For instance, Main and Cassidy (1988) found that the type of attachment when a child is 6 years old, can be predicted from their type of attachment when 12 months old.

An important question is to what extent differences between people stem from differences in their **heredity** (genetics), compared to differences in their environment (e.g. experiences encountered in their lives). Twin studies (see Box 6.2) allow us to assess how much heredity and environment produce these individual differences. To measure the relative contribution of heredity, researchers can use a heritability estimate, which indicates how much variance in a characteristic (in a population) is due to differences in genetic variation (see Box 6.3).

The environment we live in is classified into two types: shared and non-shared. Shared environment is the one common to siblings brought up in the same family, which includes such aspects as similar diet, language, socio-economic status and so on. This form of environment makes those who experience it similar to a trait. However, even with a shared environment, siblings still develop into distinct characters. Non-shared (unique) environment is the one which is exclusive to that person and makes people different from, rather than similar to, their relatives. It includes such factors as childhood accidents and your own set of friends, not shared with your siblings. We will now turn to the research paper which uses a twin study to examine to what extent genes and environment contribute to individual differences in attachment types.

Box 6.2 Methods: twin studies

Twin studies aim to work out how much of a character/behaviour is due to **heredity** and how much of it is due to the environment. In twin studies, researchers recruit pairs of twins and collect data about their behaviour and/or characteristics. Alternatively, researchers can use existing databanks of information collected from twins. Twins can be identical or non-identical. Identical twins are also called monozygotic (MZ) twins; non-identical twins are also called dizygotic (DZ) or fraternal twins. The number of genes they have in common depends on whether they are MZ or DZ twins. MZ twins develop from the same fertilized egg, so they essentially have identical genes; they share 100 per cent of their genes. DZ twins develop from two different fertilized eggs, so they are no more similar genetically than ordinary siblings; they share 50 per cent of their genes.

Twin studies assume that because twins are raised together, both types (MZ and DZ) are affected by their environments to the same extent. As such, a factor that makes MZ twins more alike than DZ twins, must be their greater genetic similarity. This is called the equal environments assumption. Twin studies analyse the rates of similarity for MZ and DZ twins and then compare them. If it is found that MZ twins are more similar than DZ twins, it indicates a genetic influence. If similarity for both MZ and DZ twins is about the same, it indicates a shared environmental influence. When MZ twins are dissimilar, it indicates a non-shared environmental influence.

Twin studies can calculate three things:

1. Concordance rates: the proportion of twin pairs that both have the characteristic being investigated.
2. Correlation coefficients: the extent to which a measurement/score for one twin predicts the measurement/score for the second twin.
3. Heritability estimates: the relationship between the observable (**phenotypic**) variation of the trait in twin pairs and the genetic variation for those twin pairs (see Box 6.3).

 Box 6.3 Methods: heritability estimate

Psychological characteristics that are affected by genetics are said to be heritable. A heritability estimate is the estimate of how much variance in a characteristic in a population (phenotypically) is due to differences in heredity (genetic variation).

An estimate of 0 means that genetic differences account for none of the variation in a characteristic in a population. An estimate of 1 indicates that genetic differences account for all of the observed variations in characteristic in a population. The complement of heritability is 'environmentability', which is the contribution of environmental variation to phenotypic variation in a population. Heritability and environmentability for any given trait in a population together add up to 100 per cent.

Heritability applies only to groups, not to individuals, so it does not give a figure for a person's chances of inheriting a trait. For example, a heritability estimate of 0.40 indicates that, on average, about 40 per cent of the individual differences we observe in a trait *in a population*, may be attributable to genetic individual difference. It does not indicate that 40 per cent of any individual's trait is due to his/her genes.

The paper

Bokhorst, C., Bakermans-Kranenburg, M.J., Fearon, R.M.P., Van Ijzendoorn, M.H., Fonagy, P. and Schuengel, C. (2003) The importance of shared environment in mother-infant attachment security: a behavioural genetic study. *Child Development*, 74: 1769–82.

Abstract

In a sample of 157 monozygotic and dizygotic twins, genetic and environmental influences on infant attachment and temperament were quantified. Only unique environmental or error components could explain the variance in disorganized versus organized attachment, as assessed in the Ainsworth Strange Situation Procedure. For secure versus non-secure attachment, 52% of the variance in attachment security was explained by shared environment, and 48% of the variance was explained by unique environmental factors and measurement error. The role of genetic factors in attachment disorganization and attachment security was negligible. Genetic factors explained 77% of the variance in temperamental reactivity, and unique environmental factors and measurement error explained 23%. Differences in temperamental reactivity were not associated with attachment concordance.

This abstract states how the authors use identical (monozygotic) and non-identical (dizygotic) twins to look at how much of the type of attachment between child and parent, and temperament, is due to either genes or environment. They then summarize the findings; do not worry if you do not understand all of the terms here, as they are explained in the rest of this commentary.

Introduction

Behavioural genetic research on twins, siblings, and unrelated (adoptive or step) children have changed our views on child development drastically . . . It has been argued that there is an urgent need to rethink radically the role of parents in child development . . . Considering the amount of evidence in favour of a major role for genetics in the development of behaviours, personality traits, and attitudes, one is inclined to emphasize the influences of genetics and unique environmental pressures more heavily than in the past. In a summary of the advances of behaviour genetic research, McGuffin *et al.* (2001) stated that . . . most behaviours that have been studied show moderate to high heritability, and if environment plays a role, its contribution often is non-shared or unique because it makes people different from, instead of similar to, their relatives . . . Parental behaviour that stimulates similar developmental patterns across siblings (shared environment) seems to be elusive, and important behaviours or characteristics without a substantial genetic component seem to be rare. Nevertheless, in several behavioural genetic studies a contribution of the shared environment has been found, in particular when they included infants and young children (Leve *et al.*, 1998 . . .). In the current study further evidence is presented for a seemingly unusual combination of a small or negligible genetic component and a large (shared or non-shared) environmental component concerning patterns of infant attachment behaviour.

Previous research evidence is used in this first part of the introduction, to set the scene for this research. Behavioural genetic research studies the contributions of environmental (nurture) and genetic (nature) factors to individual variations in human behaviour. The authors state that evidence from behavioural genetic research suggests that parents have less influence on a child's development than genetics. Much evidence indicates that genes contribute to many behaviours and, if environment is a factor, it is of the kind that makes people dissimilar from each other (unique/non-shared environment) rather than the kind that makes people similar (shared environment). Thus, previous research shows a large genetic contribution and a small environmental one. However, some studies do show that the shared environment contributes to behaviour, especially for infants and young children. This study gives further evidence for an unusual pattern of a large environmental contribution and a small genetic, one by looking at types of attachment in infants.

From attachment theory, strong predictions about the role of shared environment in the development of organized infant attachment strategies may be derived (Main, 1999). Attachment theory stresses the influence of parental attachment representations and parenting behaviour (O'Connor *et al.*, 2000; O'Connor and Croft, 2001) . . . Secure, resistant, and avoidant attachment behaviour patterns (Ainsworth *et al.*, 1978) are thought to result from the infants' experiences with (in)consistently sensitive or consistently insensitive parents . . . This seems to imply a large role for the shared environment, not only for attachment security but also for the organized non-secure attachment patterns, that is, resistant and avoidant attachment.

Attachment theory considers parental behaviour (e.g. parental sensitivity) to be a factor in the development of organized attachment. Parental behaviour is part of the shared environment. For example, it is suggested that parents who respond sensitively, being warm and giving loving responses to the child, produce securely attached children. 'Parental attachment representations' are the parent's own mental concept of what close relationships are like. 'Organized' attachment is explained in Box 6.1.

The transmission of attachment from parents to their infants may nevertheless at least be partly mediated by a genetic pathway (Main, 1999). Although several studies have provided support for . . . parental attachment representations [and] parental sensitivity [on] infant attachment strategy (Main *et al.*, 1985), a large and quantifiable transmission gap of about 75% of the intergenerational transmission remains to be closed (Van Ijzendoorn, 1995b [1995]) . . . Several attempts to close the gap have been made by assessing attachment security and parental sensitivity during long observational sessions in the natural setting . . . Nevertheless, the transmission gap could not be closed this way.

Of course, genetics seems a plausible candidate for closing the transmission gap because parents and infants share 50% of their genes, and intergenerational transmission of attachment may (partly) be based on transmission of genes from one generation to the next. More specifically, behaviour genetic studies have documented that a large part of individual differences in the affective quality of parent-child relationships is influenced by active **genotype**-environment interactions (O'Connor and Croft, 2001). For example, genetic differences in temperament may provoke different environmental reactions, and may lead to diverging attachment behaviour patterns. The genetic transmission of temperament may thus be partly responsible for the link between parent and infant attachment, and it may account for part of the transmission gap. In the current study, the heritability of temperament was investigated, and it was tested whether similarities in temperamental reactivity between twins are associated with concordance in attachment relationships to the same caregiver.

Here the authors state the alternative to environmental influence, which is that genes contribute to attachment rather than the environment. Some evidence suggests that there is not a direct link between a parent's attachment representation and the child's attachment (e.g. it is not always the case that a secure parent has a secure child). As such, there is still a substantial unexplained part called the transmission gap. This is the gap between parents' attachment representation and their infant's attachment type. The researchers consider what factors may close the transmission gap. One possibility is that the infant inherits their temperament, which affects how they relate to others and how others relate to them, leading to differing attachment styles ('affective' means 'emotional'). In this study, they will examine the heritability of temperament (i.e. how much it is inherited) and how much twins having similar temperaments relates to them having the same attachment type.

> In a previous study on similarity of attachment in siblings (Van Ijzendoorn *et al.*, 2000) some evidence was found for the idea that mothers stimulate similar attachment relationships with siblings . . . [but] the role of (shared and non-shared) environment was still confounded with the role of genetics because contrast groups with varying degrees of genetic relatedness were lacking. It was therefore impossible to address the question of heritability of attachment with a behaviour genetic approach. Twin studies provide a unique opportunity to test the similarity of siblings' attachment relationships under conditions of similar age and childrearing contexts, using established behaviour genetic methods. Few studies have been performed on the attachment relationships of twins, and these have tended to involve relatively small samples . . . [for example] Ricciuti (1992) found 78% concordance of attachment security in 27 dizygotic (DZ) twin pairs and 66% concordance in 29 monozygotic (MZ) twin pairs: she therefore concluded that in this combined sample of 12- to 22-month-old twins, attachment security as assessed through the Strange Situation did not show genetic influence . . .

Research indicates that mothers have a similar type of attachment with each sibling. However, it is hard to tell if this is due to shared environment or to genetics, as parents and children share both environment and genes. So, there is a need to use twin studies to distinguish between these. Concordance is the proportion of twin pairs that both have the characteristic being investigated (e.g. both have type A attachment). Previous research has found that MZ twins are not more similar in attachment security than DZ twins. When the concordance rate for MZ twins exceeds that for DZ twins, it indicates a genetic influence; when concordance rates are similar for both MZ and DZ twins, it indicates a shared environmental influence.

> The current study focused separately on disorganized attachment defined as the (sometimes momentary) breakdown of the organized strategy to deal with stress (Main and Solomon, 1990) and on the organized attachment patterns (secure, avoidant and resistant) as presented in Ainsworth *et al.* (1978). Traditional family research presupposes that parental sensitivity as part of the (non)shared environment is an important determinant of attachment security or non-security (DeWolff and Van Ijzendoorn, 1997). Thus, the influence of a genetic component on the organized attachment strategies was expected to be small. With respect to the disorganized attachment group, the empirical evidence does not unequivocally suggest a major role for the shared environment. Some observational studies without a behavioural genetic design confirmed the role of . . . parenting in the emergence of disorganization ([e.g.] Van Ijzendoorn *et al.*, 1999). In contrast, Spangler *et al.* (1996) found that attachment disorganization was best predicted by newborn behavioural organization in terms of orienting ability and regulation of state instead of parenting. Furthermore, [an] investigation found some evidence for the role of the dopamine D4 receptor (DRD4) gene polymorphism ([e.g.] Lakatos *et al.*, 2000). Therefore, diverging genetic mechanisms may determine the development of disorganized and organized attachment patterns, and separate hypotheses and subsequent analyses are warranted.
>
> In sum, the following hypotheses were tested. First . . . we expected a role for a genetic component in disorganized attachments . . . Second, we expected that individual differences in organized patterns of attachment behaviour would show a substantial influence of the shared environment. Our main hypothesis concerned attachment security versus non-security, which constitutes the basic split in attachment classifications (Ainsworth *et al.*, 1978). Our third hypothesis concerned the heritability of temperamental reactivity. Temperamental reactivity was expected to be highly genetically influenced . . . We also tested whether temperamental similarities were responsible for concordance in attachment classifications (Van Ijzendoorn, 1995b [1995]; Fearon, 1999).

The current study investigates organized attachment separately from disorganized attachment (organized attachment includes secure, insecure ambivalent and insecure avoidant types). Previous research suggests that the environment is important in organized attachment (secure and non-secure), so they expect only a small genetic influence on organized attachments. For disorganized attachment, it is not clear cut whether environmental or genetic factors are more important. One possible genetic factor is the type of dopamine gene. Dopamine is a chemical that occurs naturally in the brain and carries messages between brain cells. It is involved in many functions, such as emotion and movement. The receptor is the part of the brain cell that receives dopamine. There are several kinds of receptor that receive dopamine, one being the D4 receptor.

The researchers' hypotheses predict:

1   A genetic role for disorganized attachment.
2   A role for shared environment on organized attachment (they also examine environmental and genetic contributions to secure and insecure attachment).
3   A genetic role in temperament (they also test if similarity in temperament in twin pairs is responsible for both twins showing the same type of attachment).

Method

Participants
Participants came from two twin studies . . . The two studies used similar designs and measures.

   The Leiden twin study. The sample consisted of 76 twin pairs, with 27 MZ and 40 DZ same sex pairs. The families were recruited through the Netherlands Twin Register . . . which contains 40% to 50% of all multiple births after 1986 . . . Most families were middle class . . . The mean age of the mothers was 32 years (SD = 3.6). The children were observed in Ainsworth's Strange Situation Procedure when they were between 12 and 14 months of age . . . The two children of the same twin pair were seen separately, with an intervening period of one week. *The London twin study*. The sample consisted of 62 same sex twin pairs, with 30 MZ and 32 DZ twin pairs, living in and around London . . .

Design and procedure
All infants were observed in Ainsworth's Strange Situation Procedure for assessment of mother-child attachment (Ainsworth *et al.*, 1978). In both studies, the mothers were asked to assess the temperament of their children by completing a questionnaire for each child separately. The mothers of the Leiden twins received the Infant Behaviour Questionnaire (IBQ; Rothbart, 1981) at home 2 months before they came to the laboratory. The mothers of the London twins were asked to complete the Infant Characteristics Questionnaire (Bates *et al.*, 1979) at home 2 months before the Strange Situation assessment.

It is important that the Leiden and London studies had similar designs and measures, as this ensures that they are comparable. This section describes the attributes of the sample. For example, the authors mention the families' social class and educational level. This is necessary as the findings may differ for different classes and educational levels. It also means that they can be reliably compared to other studies which used similar class and educational levels. As for the Leiden study, they do give details of the London sample to show that they are similar (these are not included here for brevity).

> *Measures*
> *Strange Situation Procedure*. The well-known and standard Strange Situation Procedure was used to assess infant-mother attachment security in both samples. The procedure consists of three stressful components: the infant enters with the mother to an unknown laboratory playroom; a stranger comes in and tries to play with the infant; the mother leaves the room twice for a brief period. In particular, infants' behaviour at reunion with the mother is essential for coding the quality of the attachment relationship . . . In all studies, strange situations were coded by experienced coders who reached satisfactory **intercoder reliability** . . .

Measures are the dependent variables (i.e. how they are assessing/scoring the children's behaviour). See Box 6.1 for a description of the Strange Situation. It is important that they use a standard procedure which has been tested before. This also allows for comparison across studies. Using experienced coders should mean that they obtain reliable scores.

> *Temperamental reactivity*. In the Leiden twin sample, the Infant Behaviour Questionnaire (Rothbart, 1981) was used. The IBQ is an instrument designed to assess temperament by asking caregivers about particular behaviours of infants. Caregivers are asked to respond to most items on the basis of the behaviour of the infant during the previous week . . . The IBQ consists of six subscales: Activity Level, Smiling and Laughter, Fear Distress to Limitations, Soothability, and Vocal Activity. A seventh scale, Overall Reactivity, was computed . . .

The researchers are using a mixture of research methods; the Strange Situation involves an observation research method and they use two standard pre-tested questionnaires, to assess children's temperaments. The researchers do also describe the London questionnaire but it is not included here for brevity.

> *Zygosity determination* In the Leiden sample, Zygosity was determined with the Zygosity Questionnaire for Young Twins (Goldsmith, 1991). This

questionnaire was completed three times by the mother: at 10 months of age, at 12 months of age, and at 3 years of age. Questions concern similarities of physical features of the twins and experiences of mistaking one twin for another . . . For a substantial number of the London twins information about placentation was available; this way 47% of these twins were identified as MZ. For the other twins, Zygosity was determined using a genetic test (Freeman *et al.*, 1997). Parents were given a test kit . . . They were asked to take the DNA samples of their twins (a sample of cheek cells) at home and to send them to Freeman's laboratory for Zygosity determination.

Zygosity refers to whether twins are identical (MZ), having developed from the same egg, or non-identical (DZ), where they are from two different eggs. Sometimes identical twins can have physical differences, appearing non-identical and vice versa. The Zygosity questionnaire checks that the twins really are MZ or DZ, as this would affect the findings. Placentation refers to the **placenta**; generally MZ twins shared one placenta and DZ twins had one each. The genetic test can be used, as MZ twins share 100 per cent of their genes, whereas DZ twins share 50 per cent of their genes.

Statistical analysis
After presenting basic descriptive data . . . the simple percentages of concordance of MZ and DZ twin pairs for disorganized and secure attachment classifications are first provided. These percentages were obtained by dividing the number of concordant pairs (e.g. both infants secure or, both infants non-secure) by the total number of twin pairs . . . For genetic modelling . . . the raw frequencies of classifications for MZ twins and DZ twins were inserted . . . The genetic analyses were performed with the program Mx (Neale *et al.*, 1999) . . . we differentiated two levels of data analysis. This first level concerned disorganized attachment [versus] organized secure and non-secure attachment strategies . . . On the second level, only twin pairs were included that were both classified as attached in an organized way. Thus, the second and most important level in the current investigation concerned the split of the organized attachments into secure and non-secure classifications . . .

This section describes what analysis was done; the researchers calculated concordance rates (see Box 6.2) and conducted genetic modelling. This modelling works out the relative contributions of genetic and environmental factors to a trait.

Results

Distributions and concordances of attachment: Descriptive outcomes
. . . For MZ twins, the percentages of concordance were 72% for disorganized versus organized (D-nonD) attachment and 56% for secure
versus non-secure (B-nonB) attachment; for DZ twins, the concordances
were 73% for D-nonD attachment and 60% for B-nonB attachment . . .
These percentages stressed the importance of the environment, not only
for disorganized and secure attachment but also for the avoidant and the
resistant attachment classifications.

*Modelling genetic, shared, and non-shared environmental components
in attachment*
In behavioural genetic analyses, the similarity of pairs of twins is
decomposed into similarity due to additive genetic factors (A) and similarity due to shared environmental experiences (C), and dissimilarity is
accounted for by unique or non-shared environmental influences and
measurement error (E). The genetic analyses were performed with the
program Mx . . . which provides estimates of the parameters in the ACE
model (A, genetic factors; C, shared environment; E, non-shared environment and measurement error) and an overall chi-square goodness-of-fit
index. A small chi-square corresponds to good fit, and a large chi-square
corresponds to bad fit . . .

Role of temperament
Means and standard deviations on temperamental reactivity . . . for the
four attachment categories are presented . . . The difference in correlations [for temperamental reactivity] between MZ and DZ twins pointed
to a genetic component. The important role of genetics in temperamental reactivity was supported by the results of modelling . . . The
association among temperamental reactivity and the four-way attachment
classifications was not significant . . .

For simplicity, the results section has been abridged. To summarize, the findings shown here are:

1   Concordance rates suggest that environment is important for dis-
    organized and organized attachment.
2   For organized versus disorganized attachments, the genetic modelling
    suggests that unique environment (and measurement error) explain
    the variance in disorganization.

3   For secure versus non-secure attachments, the model suggests that 52 per cent of variance in attachment security is explained by shared environment influences and 48 per cent of variance is explained by unique environment (and measurement error).

4   The modelling suggests that genetic factors explain 77 per cent of the variance in temperamental reactivity, and unique environment (and measurement error) explains 23 per cent.

5   They found that temperament appears to be genetic, but did not predict the concordance in attachment types of twins.

Discussion

. . . The current behavioural genetic study found considerable evidence to support the decisive role of environmental factors in the development of (non)secure attachment, with concordances for MZ and DZ twins that leave some room for shared and unique environmental influences. Behaviour genetic modelling indicates that the heritability of disorganized and secure attachment behaviour is negligible. The unique environment seems responsible for disorganization of attachment, and the shared environment counts for more than half of the variance in secure attachment. This not only represents confirmation of one of the basic assumptions of attachment theory but also seems to fit well with research that has documented a robust association between maternal representations of attachment and infant attachment security . . .

In an age when shared environmental theories of development have been rejected by some behaviour-geneticists . . . the finding of a substantial shared environment influence is noteworthy . . . A noteworthy finding from this investigation of attachment in families with twins is the substantial influence of non-shared environmental factors, in particular, in the development of disorganized attachment . . . some non-shared influences on different infants within the same family may be triggered by differences in temperament between the siblings. However, in our twin study it was not possible to trace any effect of temperamental (dis)similarity on the concordance of attachment . . .

The current findings fail to support the hypothesis that the so-called transmission gap might be closed by genetic factors . . . The search for mechanisms that help close the transmission gap may now concentrate on parenting behaviours different from the classic sensitivity concept . . . but, maybe more important, also on unique environmental factors shaping the infant's patterns of attachment behaviour . . . we are currently collecting DNA samples from the twins involved in our investigation to test whether behavioural-genetic and molecular-genetic approaches, in the same participants, show converging evidence.

In future studies, it is also important to include parenting in the modelling of genetic and environmental components of attachment . . . [For example] In search for the meaning of the (non)shared environment in the emergence of attachment security, parental sensitivity as assessed in interactions with both children of a twin pair may be crucial. This approach might show that the unique environment (partly) consists of parental behaviour that intentionally or accidentally differentiates the developmental pathways of both children within a twin pair . . . Longitudinal studies on parental sensitivity and attachment in twins, siblings, and unrelated children, may open exciting avenues for uncovering the interplay among genes, shared environment, and non-shared environment in children's socioemotional development.

The researchers found that environment is a factor in organized attachment (secure and non-secure) and that there is little contribution of genetic factors for disorganized or secure attachment. Instead, unique environment is a factor in disorganized attachment, and shared environment is a factor in secure attachment. As these findings support attachment theory and previous research, they are important in that they show that the trend for emphasizing genetic factors, as more important than environment is not true for all behaviours. This commentary has been abridged where they consider explanations, such as measurement error and so on. They go on to suggest a need for more research and provide suggestions for this.

Summary of Bokhorst *et al.* (2003)

This research examined the individual differences in the types of attachment (emotional bond) infants have with their mother. Bokhorst and colleagues examined how much genes and/or environment contribute to these differences in attachment types in a population. Using a twin study and the Strange Situation observation, they found that environment does play an important part in differences in attachment, whereas genetics plays only a small role. For example, they found that environmental factors that make people similar (shared environment), contribute to 52 per cent of the difference between infants for secure versus insecure attachment, whereas environmental factors that make people dissimilar (non-shared environment), contribute to 48 per cent of this difference. Behavioural genetic research is a rapidly expanding area of research. However, a general problem with examining heritability is that it can only tell us about the population being studied, in one particular environment, at one point in time.

Summary of developmental psychology

We have looked at the area of developmental psychology which investigates our behaviour at different ages and how our behaviour changes over time. This area benefits from using a diverse range of research methods to study development, such as laboratory experiments, observations, and cross-sectional and longitudinal studies. What has been learnt from research in this area, has been successfully applied to real world situations. For example, evidence from research into cognitive development has been used to enhance how children learn in the classroom. Likewise, understanding of attachments has been used to train parents to be more sensitive to children's behaviours in order to increase the chances of the child forming secure attachments (e.g. to help adoptive parents form attachments with a child). Box 6.4 gives some summaries of other research in developmental psychology. These summaries are drawn from the whole range of developmental psychology, focusing on different life stages. One piece of research is on the effects of being a grandparent and the other is on young girls' awareness of dieting and unhappiness with their bodies.

 Box 6.4 Research: other research in developmental psychology

Kaufman and Elder (2003): Grandparenting and age identity
What makes one person who is 70 years old feel 60, whereas another 70-year-old can feel 80? People of the same age can feel different ages (their age identity), regardless of their actual age. Kaufman and Elder (2003) were interested in what makes people feel different ages. They suggested that being a grandparent may play a role in people's age identity, as becoming a grandparent marks a new stage in life and is associated with being older. They examined whether those who enjoy being a grandparent have a younger age identity than those who do not enjoy it, and whether those who become a grandparent early in life think of themselves as older than those who become a grandparent 'on time'. They questioned 666 grandparents living in a rural region of the USA, using phone interviews and posted questionnaires. They specifically examined four aspects of age: what age they would be if they could choose any age (desired age); what age they feel most of the time (subjective age); what age they hope to live to (desired longevity); and at what age they consider people to become old (perceived old age).

They found that being a grandparent does affect people's age identity. Those who enjoy being a grandparent feel younger, perceive old age to begin later and hope to live longer. For example, a 70-year-old woman who does not enjoy being a grandparent feels their age, considers old age to being at around 68 years and hopes to live to 78 years. In contrast, a 70-year-old woman who enjoys being a grandparent feels about 61 years old, sees old age as beginning nearer 76 years old and hopes to live to 84 years. They also found that men wish to be about five years younger than women do (desired age). Those people who became grandparents early in life feel older than those on time.

*Dohnt and Tiggemann (2005): How **peers** affect young girls' dissatisfaction with their bodies*

It is known that adolescents are influenced by their peers when it comes to satisfaction with their bodies and dieting, but is this also the case for young girls? In their study, Dohnt and Tiggemann (2005) explored how peers influence the development of body dissatisfaction (e.g. wanting to be thinner) and awareness of dieting in girls from 5 to 7 years old. Peers are an important source of information for young children. Peers may influence body dissatisfaction and dieting awareness by having, for example, shared group **norms** about dieting or believing that being thinner will make them more liked by their peers. To examine this issue, the researchers individually interviewed 81 girls (in Australia) who were in reception, Year 1 and Year 2 at school (mean ages 5.18 years, 6.12 years and 7.11 years respectively). They measured body dissatisfaction, dieting awareness, perceptions of peers' body dissatisfaction, awareness of teasing and likeability based on weight, peer discussion about body shape and being accepted by peers. For instance, for body dissatisfaction, the girls were asked to point to silhouettes of nine young female bodies ranging from very thin (1) to very fat (9). They were asked to point to the girl most like themselves and the girl they would most like to look like. Body dissatisfaction was scored as the difference between these two. Their perception of their peers' body dissatisfaction was measured by, for example, being asked to point to the figure that most of the girls in their class would like to look like.

They found that a substantial number (46.9 per cent) of young girls want to be thinner and were aware of dieting as a way of getting thinner. This developed over time; reception-aged girls showed little body dissatisfaction but, by Year 2, 71.4 per cent of the girls wanted to be thinner. Dieting awareness also increased with age. They found that, as with adolescents, awareness of teasing and likeability was linked to dieting behaviour. However, unlike adolescents, peer discussions and acceptance, were not related to body dissatisfaction and dieting awareness in young girls. Their major new finding was that the girls' perception of their peers' body dissatisfaction was related to their own level of body dissatisfaction.

7 Biological psychology

In this chapter, we look at what biological psychology is and then examine one research paper in detail.

- The area: biological psychology views the way we behave in terms of our biology, that is, how our body works.
- The research: does the size of our brains relate to how clever we are?

What is biological psychology?

Biological psychology is concerned with how biological processes (e.g. the workings of the brain) relate to our mental functions and behaviour (e.g. sleep, memory, emotion). It considers the physical basis of our thoughts, feelings and behaviours. It takes into account how the nervous system works (which includes the brain), how hormones affect our behaviour, the effect of our genes and so on.

The subject area of biological psychology has been of interest for a long time! For instance, the ancient Greek physician and philosopher Galen, suggested that personality and temperament were related to body fluids (e.g. blood, bile). Descartes (1596–1650) made the distinction between the human mind and human body, arguing that the mind is completely separate from the body. From the late 1600s, it has been understood that the brain is the biological base of psychological phenomena. However, at that time it was hard to understand how the brain worked and the various functions of the different areas of the brain. Our understanding of the relationship between our biology and our psychology has increased as our knowledge of how the body works has advanced. Milestones in our understanding include, for example, Broca's discovery (1861) of one of the brain areas responsible for speech in humans and Fritsch and Hitzig's (1870) detection of the brain's motor regions, found by electrically stimulating the **cortex**. More recently, advancing methods for scanning the brain, such as **magnetic resonance imaging**, mean that we can monitor brain activity **non-invasively**. Our understanding is still progressing along with the development of technology (e.g. the development of more refined scanning methods, such as the **magnetoencephalogram**).

Research in biological psychology uses such methods as laboratory experiments and observations, as well as calculating correlations between twins and adopted people, to understand how genes affect behaviour. The research paper which we look at in this chapter, uses a method called meta-analysis which draws together findings of previous research studies (see Box 7.1). The paper examines if the size of our brains (part of our biology) relates to how clever we are (part of our behaviour).

Research paper

McDaniel published the findings from his meta-analysis in *Intelligence* journal in 2005. He conducted a meta-analysis to pull together and analyse previous

 Box 7.1 Methods: meta-analysis

Meta-analysis is the statistical analysis of a collection of individual studies. Glass (1976) first established this method of integrating the findings of previous research. It is useful for all areas of psychology, not just biological psychology. Meta-analysis is used to combine the data from many previous research studies, summarize it and review it. It gives a systematic overview, combining all research on one topic into one large 'study'. As it is a form of reviewing much research that has examined the same question, it can be used to settle controversies from conflicting studies.

When doing a meta-analysis, the researcher(s) must make a judgement about what studies to include. The dependent variable is the effect size which provides information about how much change there is across studies (magnitude of effects) and the direction of effects across studies. There are two types of effect size: correlation and standardized mean difference. We will focus on correlation as this is relevant to the research paper in this chapter (see Chapter 2 for an explanation of correlation). A correlation looks at the strength of association between two variables; in our case, one variable is brain size and the other variable is intelligence. To obtain an effect size (for correlations), the analysis codes the features of the study, transforms these study outcomes to a common metric so outcomes can be compared and uses statistical methods to show the relationship between the study features and outcomes.

studies which investigated the link between brain size and intelligence. Before we look at this paper in detail, we will briefly review intelligence and brain size.

Background: intelligence and brain size

What exactly is intelligence? It is difficult to state what it is as there is no one formal definition. The term 'intelligence' is generally used to refer to a range of mental abilities, such as the capacity to understand complex ideas, plan, solve problems, learn new abilities and to use abstract thinking. Although different researchers and theories emphasize some of these abilities over others, it is agreed that intelligence is not one thing but is a number of factors. For example, Spearman (1863–1945) suggested that there is general intelligence (called the g-factor or 'g') and various specific intelligences (s-factors). Various intelligence tests have been devised to measure a person's intelligence (see Box 7.2).

The brain is the seat of everything that we do, feel, remember and so on. The brain of the average adult human weighs 1.3 to 1.4kg (about 3 pounds), is 14 cm wide, 16.7cm long and 9.3cm high and represents about two per cent of total body weight. Whether having a larger brain makes you more intelligent has long been debated. For example, in 1888, Sir Francis Galton published evidence which appeared to confirm a link between brain size and intelligence. He had measured the head sizes of two classes of students. Those in the higher-ability class had larger head sizes than those in the lower-ability class, by almost five per cent.

Advances in technology have led to a renewal in interest in this relationship. Researchers nowadays benefit from having better methods to measure brain size than just external measures (e.g. head dimensions). We can now measure brain size **in vivo** using such non-invasive methods as magnetic resonance imaging (MRI) and so on. Recent research evidence indicates that brain size does relate to intelligence, but more so for some aspects of intelligence than others, and this relationship differs for women and men. Such factors as sex and age need to be considered, as these relate to the organization of the brain. For example, men's brains are larger than women's, but women's brains decrease in size less with age than men's do.

The paper

McDaniel, M.A. (2005) Big-brained people are smarter: a meta-analysis of the relationship between in vivo brain volume and intelligence. *Intelligence*, 33: 337–46.

᠅ **Box 7.2** Methods: measuring intelligence

Various tests (measures) have been developed to gauge a person's intelligence. Intelligence tests measure performance in specific areas (e.g. verbal ability, memory or reasoning). The most common measure is the intelligence quotient (IQ) which gives a score in points; the higher the score, the more intelligent the person. The average IQ is 100. All intelligence tests are standardized tests. They are pretested on a group of people representative of the whole population and then graded so that the majority of people will get between 90 and 110. An individual's score can then be compared against other peoples' scores. The group scores produce a **normal distribution curve**. On this curve, there are as many scores above the mean (average) as below it. Most scores cluster around the mean, with fewer scores as it moves away from the mean (i.e. there are few people at the extremes of low and high IQ).

Binet and Simon (1905) developed the first successful test known as the 'Binet-Simon Intelligence Scale'. Other tests include the Weschler Intelligence Scales and the British Ability Scales. The research paper in this chapter mentions the Ravens Progressive Matrices Test. This test measures the ability to make sense of complex data and to perceive new relationships, and to store and reproduce information. It emphasizes nonverbal intellectual ability. In each test item, the person is asked to find a missing pattern in a sequence of patterns with each set of items getting progressively harder.

Intelligence tests do have their problems. For instance, most intelligence tests are concerned with only a narrow set of skills and may only measure the ability to take the tests! Also, intelligence tests do not account for all factors that influence a person's success in life, such as motivation, attitudes and so on.

Abstract

The relationship between brain volume and intelligence has been a topic of a scientific debate since at least the 1830s. To address the debate, a meta-analysis of the relationship between in vivo brain volume and intelligence was conducted. Based on 37 samples across 1530 people, the population correlation was estimated at 0.33. The correlation is higher for females than males. It is also higher for adults than children. For all age and sex groups, it is clear that brain volume is positively correlated with intelligence.

'Samples' refers to the previous research studies used in the meta-analysis. A correlation of 0.33 is a positive relationship, which means that high scores on one variable are associated with high scores on another variable (see Chapter 2).

Introduction

In 1836, Frederick Tiedmann wrote that there exists 'an indisputable connection between the size of the brain and the mental energy display by the individual man' (as cited in Hamilton, 1935). Since that time, the quest of the biological basis of intelligence has been pursued by many. Various narrative reviews (Rushton and Ankney, 1996) . . . and a meta-analysis (Nguyen and McDaniel, 2000) have documented a non-trivial positive relationship between brain volume and intelligence in non-clinical samples. In the brain volume literature, there are two general categories of brain volume measures. The first category consists of measures of the external size of the head, such as the circumference of the head. The second category consists of measures of the in vivo brain volume, typically assessed through an MRI scan. For external head measures, Vernon *et al.* (2000) reported the population correlation between head size and intelligence to be 0.19. Nguyen and McDaniel (2000) reported population correlations from 0.17 to 0.26 for three different sub-categories of external head size measures. Studies assessing the correlation between in vivo brain volume and intelligence are more rare. Vernon *et al.* (2000) reported data on 15 such correlations and obtained a population correlation of 0.33. Nguyen and McDaniel (2000) reported the same population correlation based on 14 correlations. Gignac *et al.* (2003) reported data published in 2000, or earlier, with a mean correlation of 0.37. Since 2000, much more data relating brain volume and intelligence have become available due to the increased use of MRI-based brain assessments. The purpose of this meta-analysis is to cumulate our knowledge, concerning the magnitude of the correlation between in vivo brain volume and intelligence, in order to answer the long-standing question of this topic. In addition, potential sex and age moderators of the relationship are evaluated.

A narrative review is an expert opinion, or a thesis, where research results are interpreted in a narrative as opposed to a systematic review (such as meta-analysis) which is quantitative and aims to take into account all available evidence. 'Non-clinical samples' are those that come from people who do not have a brain disorder or brain damage. In this paper, McDaniel is specifically focusing on in vivo measures, not external measures. A moderator is a factor that alters the relationship between other variables (e.g. age may moderate the relationship between brain size and intelligence).

Methods

Literature review
A review of all known past literature was conducted using PsychInfo [sic] and Medline, as well as **citation** index searches of popular past reviews. Studies containing relevant data were reviewed to identify citations to other relevant research. Often, studies were found in which the authors collected MRI-assessed brain volume and intelligence data but did not report the correlation between these measures, because the correlation between brain volume and intelligence was not the focus of the study, and/or because the publication standards for the journal did not require a correlation matrix among all variables. For such studies, the correlations were requested from the authors. After preliminary findings were obtained, over 50 authors were contacted who: a) had published in the area of brain volume and intelligence, b) had provided commentaries on such literature, or c) were known to have an interest in the relation between brain volume and intelligence. These researchers were provided with the preliminary findings and were asked to scan the references to determine if any relevant research had been omitted. These researchers were also asked if they knew of any data sets containing both MRI-assessed brain volume and intelligence, that might be relevant to the study.

This section describes how the researcher found and selected the past research studies. PsychInfo and Medline are electronic databases which list published literature (e.g. research papers). PsychInfo provides information about literature for psychology and social, behavioural and health sciences, ranging from 1806 to present. Medline contains information relevant to the biomedical and life sciences. A correlation matrix is a table which shows the correlation coefficients between all variables.

Decision rules
The analysis included all correlations between in vivo measures of full brain volume and intelligence that met the decision rules. It did not include studies if they only measured partial brain volume, for example only frontal grey matter (Thompson *et al.*, 2001). All intelligence measures were standardized tests of general cognitive ability and primarily were full-scale IQ [**intelligence quotient**] measures or the *Ravens Progressive Matrices Test*. We did not include data from studies that estimated full-scale IQ from other measures, such as the New Adult Reading Test. Some studies reported data on more than one sample. Only one correlation between brain volume and intelligence for a given sample was reported, but whenever possible, data were coded separately by age

(children v adults) and by sex. Thus, if a sample recorded a correlation for all members of the sample and correlations separately by sex, the correlation for each sex group was included, but the correlation for all members in the sample was not included. Therefore, all correlations contributing to the meta-analysis are from independent samples. All sample members were non-clinical. Often the sample was the non-clinical control group in a clinical study.

Whereas the Gignac et al. (2003) paper is the most recently published review on this topic, it is useful to compare that data set with the data set used in this study. This paper incorporates 23 additional samples raising the total number of coefficients available for analysis from 14 to 37. Some of the 23 sample difference, is due to differing decision rules. For this paper, correlations are reported separately by sex for six studies . . . [lists them] while Gignac et al. reported a single correlation for males and females combined for five of the studies, and did not include data from Ivanovic et al. (2004). This reduced the number of different samples to 18. Gignac et al. included data from 96 individuals (Pennington et al., 2000), of whom at least half had reading disabilities. This sample was excluded from the present study because it did not meet this paper's decision rules for clinically normal subjects. Also, Gignac et al. had included a study by Tramo et al. (1998). That study was excluded from the present analysis because it lacked a measure of full brain volume. This increased the number of unique samples in this study to 20. These 20 coefficients from independent samples were drawn from 11 sources . . . [lists them] not included in the Gignac et al. review. This increased number of samples over the Gignac et al. review and the decision rule to record data separately by age and sex, permitted the evaluation of both age and sex moderators.

This section details the rules used to select the studies to be included in the meta-analysis. 'Frontal grey matter' refers to the grey matter of one of the brain's four lobes (the other lobes are the temporal, parietal and occipital lobes). The frontal lobe is at the front of the brain (above the eyes). Grey matter is a type of brain tissue that looks grey (there is also white matter). Box 7.2 describes the Ravens Progressive Matrices Test.

Analysis approach
The psychometric meta-analysis approach (Hunter and Schmidt, 1990, 2004) was used . . .

The psychometric approach uses all studies, regardless of their quality. The section deleted here, gives details of the analysis.

Results

The results of the analysis based on 37 correlations that met the decision criteria . . . [lists all 22 studies that correlations taken from] are reported . . . The best unbiased estimate of the population correlation between brain volume and intelligence is 0.33 . . . It is possible that the correlation between brain volume and intelligence in studies that provided standard deviations of intelligence, is systematically higher or lower than the studies that did not report standard deviations of intelligence. If this were the case, the interpolation of the standard deviations for those studies that did not report standard deviations might lead to biased estimates of the unattenuated correlation between brain volume and intelligence. To assess this potential problem, the author analysed the data partitioned by whether the standard deviation was reported in the study or whether it was interpolated. The similarity of the observed correlations (0.29 and 0.30) suggested that the studies, that reported standard deviations for intelligence, were not systematically different in their average observed correlation. Thus, it is reasonable to interpolate the missing standard deviations from the known standard deviations.

McDaniel's main finding is that there is a moderate positive correlation of 0.33 between brain size and intelligence scores (i.e. the larger the brain, the higher the score). Here, McDaniel acknowledges a possible limitation (inclusion/exclusion of standard deviations) and addresses it by doing a further analysis. This is a good example of an analysis being as rigorous as possible.

When the data were subdivided by sex, one obtains three sub-distributions: samples of males, samples of females and samples that contained both males and females. The relationship between brain volume and intelligence shows a clear sex moderator with the correlation being larger for females than males (0.40 v 0.34). For studies in which both males and females were combined in the same sample, the correlation is 0.25. Assuming this correlation is not an anomaly due to sampling error, it argues for separate reporting of results by sex. The data were then subdivided by age into adult and child samples. The analyses restricted to age alone showed no evidence of a moderating effect; however, the mixed sex samples and the uneven distribution of age across sex, clouded an effect that is evident when the data were divided hierarchically by sex and then by age. Female adult samples showed a somewhat larger population correlation than female children samples (0.41 v 0.37). Male adult samples showed a larger population correlation than male children samples (0.38 v 0.22). The hierarchical sex/age results also confirm the sex moderator. Female adult samples showed a higher population

correlation than male adult samples (0.41 v 0.38). Female children samples showed a higher population correlation than male children samples
(0.37 v 0.22) . . .

McDaniel also found that sex does moderate the relationship between brain
size and intelligence. The correlation is higher for women than for men.
Age also moderates the correlation between brain size and intelligence, the
correlation being larger for adults than children.

Discussion

This study's best estimate of the correlation between brain volume and
intelligence is 0.33. The correlation is higher for females than males. It is
higher for adults than children. Regardless of the subgroups examined,
the correlation between brain volume and intelligence is always positive.
It is very clear that brain volume and intelligence are related.

Data reporting and availability issues
There is much cause for concern regarding the reporting practises of
research in this area. Few studies reported means and standard deviations
and a zero-order correlation matrix among the variables . . . [for example]
The lack of a correlation matrix results in excluding data from this analysis
and thus increases publication bias concerns . . . Given the evidence of
age and sex moderators in these data, more research reporting results
separately by age and sex is warranted. Potential race moderators were
not examined due to the relative lack of non-Caucasians in the samples
and the failure to report correlations separately by race.

Additional research
In addition to more research with better reporting, two additional areas
deserve greater research attention. The first area is an examination of
the brain volume and intelligence relationship at a more refined level of
analysis than total brain volume. For example, although Staff's (2002)
results indicated a small negative correlation between brain volume and
intelligence, the fraction of brain volume that was grey matter was correlated 0.35 with intelligence. Likewise MacLullich *et al.* (2002) examined
the relationship between regional brain volumes (e.g. left and right
hippocampus, left and right frontal lobe, left and right temporal lobe) with
intelligence. The author had considered including in this meta-analysis,
an analysis of regional brain volumes with intelligence but there were too
few studies to analyze. The second area worthy of increased attention is

the genetic contribution to the brain volume and intelligence relationship. The research in this area is both recent and rapidly growing . . . These two research areas will help us to better understand the causal relationship between brain volume and intelligence.

The hippocampus is a banana-shaped part of the brain, in the temporal lobe, that is involved in forming long-term memories.

Conclusion

This paper contributes to the literature in three ways. First, the study more than doubles the number of unique samples that address the in vivo brain volume and intelligence relationship. Second, it also contributes by testing age and sex moderators of the relationship. The relationship is stronger for females than males and is stronger for adults than children. Finally, it resolves a 169-year-old debate. Tiedmann (1836) was correct to conclude that intelligence and brain volume are meaningfully related.

The discussion (and conclusion) section here is a good example of how this section is structured in a research paper; the findings are summarized, and then limitations and future research are discussed.

Summary of McDaniel (2005)

McDaniel (2005) did a meta-analysis to examine the association between brain size and intelligence. He used 37 correlation coefficients from previous research which had used in vivo brain measures, rather than external measures (e.g. measuring the head). His analysis of previous research found a correlation of 0.33 between brain volume and intelligence, which confirms that the bigger the brain, the higher the intelligence. He also found that people's sex and age can affect this relationship: the correlation between brain size and intelligence was higher for women than for men, and higher for adults than children. The advantages of conducting a meta-analysis are that it reviews existing research in an objective way, it can deal with a large number of studies and it can find relationships across studies that are not easily seen in normal reviews. However, meta-analysis is limited in that it depends on making some subjective judgements about which studies to include. Also the meta-analysis results may be distorted as the published studies, it is based on, tend to be ones which have statistically significant findings, rather than those that did not find anything.

Box 7.3 Research: other research in biological psychology

Whalen, Rauch, Etcoff, McInerney, Lee and Jenike (1998): Seeing faces unconsciously
Whalen and colleagues examined if a part of the brain, the **amygdala**, reacts to
emotional faces even when the person is not aware of having seen an emotional
face. They used **functional magnetic resonance imaging (fMRI)** to see
whether the amygdala was active even though the people were unaware of
seeing the emotional facial expressions. They presented their ten participants
with images on a screen inside the fMRI scanner. The images consisted of a happy
or fearful face, followed by a neutral face (showing no emotion). The participants
were not aware of seeing the emotional faces because they were presented very
quickly (for 33 ms) and followed immediately with the neutral face (for 167 ms),
which 'masked' them.

The researchers asked the participants about what they had seen. The participants commented on the expression of the neutral face, said they did not see
any happy/fearful faces and, when asked to point to faces seen, pointed only to
neutral ones. This indicates that they had not been conscious of the emotional
faces. The fMRI scans, however, did show that their amygdalae were active in
response to happy/fearful faces, even though participants reported not having
seen these faces. This research is one example of how we can be unconscious of
processing occurring in our brains and shows that the amygdala automatically
processes the emotional expressions.

Avenanti, Bueti, Galati and Aglioti (2005): Other people's pain affects us
Do we feel empathy for another person's pain just emotionally or also physically?
Avenanti and colleagues examined this using a method called **transcranial
magnetic stimulation (TMS)**. They used TMS to measure the amount of activity there was in participants' muscles when they saw videos of a syringe needle
penetrating another person's skin, a cotton bud gently pressing another person's
skin and/or a needle penetrating a tomato. When participants saw a needle entering another person's flesh, they reacted; there were automatic changes in activity
in the same part of their own body as in the part they saw pain being inflicted
on. These changes did not occur for seeing the cotton bud or the tomato. This
finding indicates that seeing pain activates nerve processing just as when you are
in pain yourself. We appear to map other people's pain onto our own body, so
that feeling another's pain is not just emotional, it is an automatic physical
experience. We empathize with other people's pain by simulating it in our own
bodies.

Summary of biological psychology

Research in biological psychology contributes knowledge to a very large range of mental phenomena and behaviours. For instance, we have a better understanding of how memory works and what the various areas of the brain do. Box 7.3 summarizes some more research in this area. One strength of the biological approach is that it is very scientific, being grounded in biology. It also provides very effective practical applications. For example, it has led to the development of drug treatments for depression and has increased our understanding of health issues (e.g. stress), the effects of shift work on sleep patterns and so on. Biological psychology is criticized for being **reductionist** and for oversimplifying human behaviour by ignoring other explanations, such as our interactions with other people and our environment.

8   Individual differences

In this chapter, we examine the area of individual differences and focus on one research paper.

- The area: the area of individual differences examines the psychological similarities and differences between people.
- The research: does our personality change or stay the same throughout adulthood?

What are individual differences?

The area of individual differences focuses on the psychology of individual people. While other areas of psychology aim to find the general 'laws' about behaviour (e.g. how memory works in most people), this area looks at how individual people differ in their own right. It examines how people are similar and how they are different in their feelings, thoughts and behaviours. Psychologists consider human behaviour to differ in five realms; personality, **psychopathology**, cognitive abilities, social attitudes and psychological interests. Researchers investigate differences in, for example, emotion, religiousness, motivation, learning, stress, health, perception, occupational choice and so on. When learning about psychology, the most commonly discussed areas are differences in personality and in intelligence. We have already looked at some individual differences in this book (for example, the research paper in Chapter 6 examined how people differ in attachment styles).

The official beginning of the psychology of individual differences is considered to be when the first centre for mental measurement, was established in 1885 by Francis Galton (1822–1911). Galton devised the first test to measure individual differences in intelligence. Similarly, Alfred Binet (1857–1911) devised tests to assess subnormal children attending schools in Paris, and set up a laboratory in 1895. The development of the area of individual differences is also largely tied in with the history of the topic of interest. For instance, personality has been contemplated since at least the times of the Ancient Greek philosophers. Hippocrates (circa 400 BC) classified people's differences into four types of temperament based on the balance of four bodily fluids. The four basic human personality types were phlegmatic (person is self-content, kind, shy, relaxed, observant), choleric (active, achiever, a leader, easily angered or bad tempered), melancholic (thoughtful, often very kind and considerate) and sanguine (optimistic, cheerful, steady, confident). In the early nineteenth century, Franz Gall proposed the theory of phrenology, in which a person's characteristics could be determined by the bumps on their skull (now known to be wrong!). Others, such as Freud and Jung, have also classified personality. More recently, Gordon Allport, Raymond Cattell and Hans Eysenck have made major contributions to theories of personality. The first personality test was devised by Robert Woodworth (1869–1962), during the First World War, in order to identify emotionally disturbed US Army recruits (called the Woodworth Personal Data Sheet).

The study of individual differences has been formalized over the past century but it is still a relatively young area of psychology. It involves a variety of research methods, the methods used being the most appropriate for the particular topic being investigated. For example, **psychometric** personality questionnaires and intelligence tests are frequently used to assess how people differ in these areas. We will now turn to one research paper on individual differences, which uses such personality questionnaires to examine how stable our personality is during our adult life.

Research paper

The research paper by Costa and McCrae (1988) examines one of the fundamental questions in personality: how stable and enduring is personality? It specifically investigates whether personality changes or stays the same as we get older in adulthood. Before we look at their research in detail, we will review what personality is and how it can be classified and measured.

Background: personality, traits and tests

It is clear that no two people are exactly the same; their personalities differ in a variety of ways. For instance, some people are outgoing, others are quiet, some are hard-working, others are lazy. We all talk about personality, but what exactly is it? Psychologists generally consider personality to be the distinct patterns of behaviour that characterize a person's response to situations. Personality is an internal part of a person's functioning which makes their behaviour different from other people's behaviour. It is also stable and consistent, being distinct from shifting moods and enduring through-out life.

There are many theories of personality; two kinds of theory are type theories and trait theories. Type theories view personality in terms of discrete categories, such as people being either **introverts** or **extraverts**. In contrast, trait theories view personality as consisting of a number of 'traits'. Traits are the basic qualities of the person that are expressed in many situations and make up their personality, such as being kind or hard-working. Traits are not considered to be discrete categories (like types) but to be continuous dimensions, where people differ in how much of each trait they have. For example, for the trait of aggressiveness, one person may have high levels (being belligerent) and another person may have low levels (being placid). There is some disagreement about what constitutes the basic set of trait dimensions. For example, Raymond Cattell (1905–1998) specifies sixteen primary traits, whereas others propose five major dimensions (see Box 8.1).

 Box 8.1 Details: the trait approach

A trait generally refers to a characteristic of someone's behaviour, such as being dependent, outgoing or anxious. The trait approach studies people's differences by identifying a set of traits and then describing people in terms of these traits. A variety of trait theories have been put forward. For example, Hans Eysenck (1916–1997) proposed that people differ on the three major trait dimensions of neuroticism, extroversion and psychoticism. We will look at two other influential trait theories, Cattell's sixteen dimensions and the Big Five.

Cattell's sixteen dimensions
Raymond Cattell (1957) proposed that there are sixteen basic personality traits. These were found by taking 18,000 trait words (adjectives) from a dictionary, and reducing these to 171 traits and then to 16 traits. This reduction was done using a technique called factor analysis, which determines factors which overlap and those which are distinctive. Each of the sixteen primary trait dimensions is defined by a pair of adjectives, at opposite ends of the dimension. The sixteen dimensions include, for instance, serious versus lively, shy versus socially bold, practical versus imaginative and traditional versus open to change. Cattell also distinguished between 'common traits', possessed by all people, and 'unique traits' which occur only in particular persons. Furthermore, he distinguished 'surface traits', which are overt traits that seem to go together, and 'source traits', which are the underlying causal factors of surface traits. Cattell's 16 Personality Factors questionnaire (16PF; Cattell *et al.*, 1970) is based on these sixteen trait dimensions.

The 'Big Five'

The Five Factor Model or the 'Big Five' is the trait theory which is supported by most research evidence to date. This theory was originated by several researchers (e.g. Fiske, 1949; Norman, 1963). Cattell's sixteen primary dimensions were reanalysed and reduced to five major trait dimensions. The 'Big Five' are Neuroticism, Extraversion, Openness to Experience, Agreeableness and Conscientiousness. These traits are commonly referred to by their initial letter: N, E, O, A and C.

- Extraversion refers to the tendency to seek stimulation and the company of others. For example, someone who is high on the extraversion dimension is talkative and outgoing, whereas someone who is low on this dimension is quiet and retiring.
- Neuroticism (also called emotional stability) is the tendency to easily experience unpleasant emotions, such as anger and anxiety.
- Agreeableness is the tendency to be good-natured, compassionate and cooperative.
- Conscientiousness is the tendency to be self-disciplined, and aim for achievement.
- Openness to Experience is the tendency to appreciate adventure and unusual ideas, and be imaginative and curious.

It is proposed that personality can be fully described in these five dimensions. These dimensions are essentially 'supertraits' which are measured by six components (or subordinate traits). For example, the six subordinate traits of Neuroticism are anxiety, hostility, depression, self-consciousness, impulsiveness and vulnerability. The Five Factor model can be measured using the NEO Personality Inventory (devised by Costa and McCrae, 1985). For example, a high Conscientiousness rating indicates a greater than average sense of responsibility and orderliness.

One way to examine differences in people's personalities is to measure their levels on a set of traits. Personality tests can be used for this purpose. Such tests identify a person's position on one or more trait dimensions, by comparing people tested under standardized conditions. Structured personality tests assess what a person is typically like, using set questions and answers. One example is the Minnesota Multiphasic Personality Inventory (see Box 8.2). Other methods of assessing personality, which are not based on trait theory, include projective tests. These are unstructured personality tests which present relatively ambiguous stimuli to individuals who respond by, for example, making up a story for a picture or describing what they see. An example is the **Rorschach ink-blot technique**. Projective tests are

Box 8.2 Methods: a structured personality test

The Minnesota Multiphasic Personality Inventory (MMPI)
The MMPI was originally formulated by Hathaway and McKinley in 1940. It is essentially a self-report inventory where the person gives answers to a series of statements. A revised version, the MMPI-2 (Butcher *et al.*, 1989), contains 566 statements (items) collated into ten major scales. These scales include, for example, depression, hysteria, social introversion and paranoia. An example of an item for the depression scale is 'I often feel that life is not worth the trouble'. Scores on a number of personality dimensions are given based on these answers. These scores can be used to make profiles of individuals and to directly compare them to other people. The MMPI was devised to test how similar a person is to people who have already been diagnosed with a disorder (e.g. paranoia). Its main use is for diagnosing mental disorders but it is also used to assess personality. The MMPI is a model for many other personality questionnaires, such as the California Psychological Inventory.

generally used in therapeutic settings rather than in mainstream personality research.

We now turn to the research paper by Paul Costa and Robert McCrae, published in 1988. Their research is based on the trait approach and uses a personality test (called an inventory) based on the 'Big Five'. They examine whether personality changes or is stable over time, specifically during adulthood. They investigate this by using longitudinal and cross-sectional methods, assessing people's personalities over a six-year period.

The paper

Costa, P.T. Jr. and McCrae, R.R. (1988) Personality in adulthood: a six-year longitudinal study of self-reports and spouse ratings on the NEO personality inventory, *Journal of Personality and Social Psychology*, 54(5): 853–63.

Abstract

Previous longitudinal studies of personality in adulthood have been limited in the range of traits examined, have chiefly made use of self-reports, and have frequently included only men. In this study, self-reports (N = 983) and spouse ratings (N = 167) were gathered on the NEO Personality

Box 8.3 Methods: the NEO Personality Inventory

The Neuroticism, Extraversion and Openness to Experience Personality Inventory (NEO-PI) was designed to measure the Big Five dimensions in normal adult personality. It has taken several forms.

NEO Personality Inventory (NEO-PI) by Costa and McCrae (1985)
This inventory is a self-report questionnaire which contains 181 items. These items measure the traits of Neuroticism, Extraversion and Openness to Experience. Individuals indicate how much they feel that the item is characteristic or representative of them on a five-point scale (from strongly disagree to strongly agree).

NEO Personality Inventory – Revised (NEO-PI-R) by Costa and McCrae (1992)
This is the revised version of the NEO-PI. The NEO-PI-R has 240 items which measure the Big Five traits and six subordinate traits of each. The revised version differs from the NEO-PI as it contains scales for Agreeableness and Conscientiousness and has some minor changes in items for the Neuroticism, Extraversion, and Openness scales. The NEO-PI-R is also available in other formats. For example, one format (Form R) is for observer-reports (e.g. for spouse ratings). Another form, called the NEO Five-Factor Inventory (NEO-FFI), is a shortened form containing 60 items which only measures the five factors.

> Inventory (Costa and McCrae, 1985b [1985]), which measures all five of the major dimensions of normal personality . . . The data support the position that personality is stable after age 30.

Longitudinal research involves studying the same people over a period of time, by assessing them at various ages (see Chapter 2). Self-reports are where the person reports or rates aspects of their behaviour, feelings and so on, themselves. Spouse ratings are where other people (spouse/partner) judge or rate the person. 'N' refers to the number of participants. The NEO Personality Inventory, based on the 'Big Five' traits, was developed by Costa and McCrae in 1985 (see Box 8.3). In this area of research, adulthood is considered to be reached at around age 30.

Introduction

Evidence in favour of the hypothesis that personality is stable in adulthood has mounted rapidly in the past decade (McCrae and Costa, 1984) . . .

Several longitudinal studies using a variety of standard questionnaires have converged on the twofold conclusion that mean levels of most personality traits neither increase nor decrease substantially in adulthood, and that individuals retain their relative standing over periods of as long as 40 years (Costa and McCrae, 1986). There are, however, two major qualifications to that generalization. First, as Finn (1986) noted, almost all studies have relied on self-reports for the assessment of personality . . . Finn recommended 'life span studies of personality in which researchers use ratings by significant others' (p. 818) to correct this deficiency. The second qualification concerns the selection of the personality variables examined. Researchers have reported stability across a wide range of personality characteristics, as measured by [for example] . . . the Minnesota Multiphasic Personality Inventory (MMPI; Leon *et al.*, 1979). It is possible, however, that important aspects of personality have been omitted from all of these inventories and that these traits show important maturational changes hitherto overlooked. Finn's (1986) results, using factors from the MMPI, suggested differential stability among the traits that he examined.

In this introduction, Costa and McCrae begin by describing the evidence to date. The evidence indicates that personality is stable in adulthood. Previous longitudinal studies suggest that (a) mean levels of traits remain roughly the same in adulthood and (b) that individuals' personalities are stable over as long as 40 years. ('Mean levels' refers to the levels of personality traits in a population; it is examined how these change over time.) However, a limitation of previous research is that most had used only self-reports and that not all traits have been assessed. They consider that some of the Big Five traits may remain stable during adulthood but others may change as people mature (in terms of biological development).

We have argued . . . that it is possible to generalize to the full range of personality traits only if a comprehensive taxonomy of personality is systematically examined. Several lines of evidence suggest that the five-factor model, consisting of Neuroticism (N), Extraversion (E), Openness to Experience (O), Agreeableness (A), and Conscientiousness (C), provides such a taxonomy . . . Each of these broad dimensions or domains of personality encompasses a variety of related traits, or facets, and a fully systematic approach to the investigation of stability and change in personality would examine a variety of traits within each of these five domains . . . it might be hypothesized that some of the five domains of personality are stable, whereas others change maturationally . . . although a variety of traits in the N and E domains have been shown to be longitudinally stable, data on stability or change in the O, A, and C domains are much more limited. . . . Because so few standard personality questionnaires contain measures of Openness, it has rarely been examined in longitudinal research. Available evidence from relevant scales suggests at least moderate stability . . . Although these scales measure aspects of personality within the domains of Openness, they cannot be considered adequate measures of the full domain. . . . Stability or change in Agreeableness and Conscientiousness must also be inferred at present from scattered findings . . . With regard to Conscientiousness, Conley (1985) reported 20-year stability coefficients ranging from .24 to .46 for self-reports and spouse ratings on his Impulse Control factor . . . Additional longitudinal data on the stability of these two domains is clearly needed, particularly because Agreeableness and Conscientiousness represent aspects of personality that are traditionally labelled *character* and thought to be the product of socialization. Finn (1986) suggested that such traits may show different patterns of stability from temperamental, biologically based traits such as Neuroticism and Extraversion.

Costa and McCrae, therefore, propose that to determine if personality is stable in adulthood, it is necessary to use spouse ratings as well as self-ratings and to use a more comprehensive taxonomy (catalogue) of traits, such as one based on the Big Five. Previous evidence about the Big Five traits shows that Neuroticism and Extraversion are stable over time but there is limited information on how stable Openness to Experience, Agreeableness and Conscientiousness are over time. Therefore, more data on stability for these is needed.

In the present study, we examined measures of all five domains in a large sample of men and women using cross-sectional, conventional longitudinal, and sequential designs: the instrument that we used was the NEO personality Inventory (NEO-PI; Costa and McCrae, 1985b [1985]). An earlier version of the test, the NEO Inventory, was administered in 1980 and provided the basis for a 6-year longitudinal study of six facet traits in each of the three domains of Neuroticism, Extraversion, and Openness. Two additional scales to measure Agreeableness and Conscientiousness, were developed from questionnaires administered in 1983, and are used in 3-year longitudinal studies of those domains. In addition, a third-person form of the three-domain NEO Inventory was administered to spouses of a subsample in 1980, and the full five-domain NEO-PI was completed by the same spouses in 1986. These data can be used in a parallel study of mean level changes and retest stability of personality as rated by significant others . . . If personality is truly stable, spouse ratings should predict self-reports across an interval of six years as well as they predict concurrent self-reports.

To summarize, in this research Costa and McCrae examine all five trait domains, using a large sample of men and women, a variety of methods (cross-sectional, longitudinal and sequential), and using self-reports as well as spouse ratings. They use the NEO Personality Inventory to assess people's mean levels and individuals' levels on the Big Five traits. If personality really is stable, spouse ratings should match self-reports both when rating at the same time as well as when rating across time (with spouse ratings also matching self-reports done six years later).

Method

Subjects
Data from two groups of subjects are analyzed in this report. Sample A consists of participants . . . who completed the NEO Inventory in 1980. A subsample of these individuals were targets for the spouse rating study. Sample B consists of individuals recruited in 1986 whose data are used in the cross-sectional and sequential analyses. *Sample A.* Subjects in Sample A were volunteer participants . . . [the sample was] composed of a predominantly White, community dwelling group of individuals, who have agreed to return for periodic biomedical and psychological testing. Most have at least a college degree and work in (or are retired from) scientific, professional, or managerial occupations . . . Although not representative of the general population in education or occupation, comparisons show that this sample does not differ markedly from a national sample with regard to the three personality dimensions of neuroticism, extraversion and openness to experience (Costa *et al.*, 1986). Complete data on the NEO Inventory were obtained from 365 men, aged 25 to 91 years (M = 57.6), and 270 women, aged 21 to 96 years (M = 52.5) in 1980. For approximately half of these subjects, both husband and wife were in the sample and both were asked to complete self-reports and spouse ratings on the NEO Inventory in 1980. Spouse ratings on the NEO Inventory were obtained in 1980 for 157 husbands, aged 26 to 89 years, and 151 wives, aged 21 to 86 years.

They used two samples. Sample A was used in a longitudinal study, whereas Sample B was used for cross-sectional and sequential studies (see Box 8.4). For simplicity in this chapter, we will concentrate only on the longitudinal study (Sample A). The researchers provide details of Sample A. Such details are important for rigour and for this study to possibly be replicated. For example, the **demographic** details allow for comparison with other groups of people; a group's demographics could make a difference to the findings.

Box 8.4 Methods: cross-sectional and sequential methods

Cross-sectional method
A cross-sectional method compares the behaviour of different age groups at one set time (e.g. comparing performance of a set of 20-year-olds with that of a set of 60-year-olds). It is a useful approach as it can conveniently cover a large age span. However, it is not able to compare the same individuals as they develop over time, so any differences in behaviour may come from differences in these people rather than from differences due to development.

Cross-sequential method
In this method, individuals born at the same time (a birth cohort) are compared at different times. Costa and McCrae (1988) give the example of a group of individuals born in 1920 and assessed in 1980 (therefore being 60-years-old), being compared with a group of individuals born in 1920 and assessed in 1986 (therefore being 66-years-old). Any differences between these groups cannot be attributed to being from different generations but can be due to being different ages.

Time-sequential method
In this method, individuals of the same age are compared at different times. Costa and McCrae (1988) give the example of 60-year-olds in 1980 being compared with 66-year-olds in 1986. Any differences may be due to generational differences but cannot be due to age as the groups are matched on age.

> *Attrition analyses.* . . . Reasons for attrition include death and disability, loss to follow-up and loss of interest in the project. . . . In general, these results suggest that attrition has probably not had a major effect on the conclusions to be drawn from these data. *Sample B.* Sample B was recruited from three sources . . . The 241 men ranged in age from 21 to 92 years (M = 62.4), the 311 women ranged in age from 19 to 93 years (M = 56.4) . . . In general, it appears that the two samples are quite comparable in demographic characteristics.

Providing details of **attrition** shows that this does not have an effect on the analysis in this research paper. They also show that Samples A and B are comparable in their demographic characteristics, which is important in order to make comparisons between the samples.

Measures and Procedure
The NEO Personality Inventory (NEO-PI, Costa and McCrae, 1985b [1985]) is a 181-item questionnaire developed through factor analysis to fit a five-dimension model of personality.

Factor analysis is a statistical test which is used to describe clusters of items in terms of those which overlap and those which are distinctly clear cut from each other. For example, someone described as talkative, overlaps with being described as gregarious. Factor analysis obtains a measurement of the common factor that seems to be shared among all of the items.

> An earlier version of the test, the NEO Inventory (McCrae and Costa, 1983), measured six traits in each of the three domains of Neuroticism (N), Extraversion (E), and Openness to Experience (O); this instrument was completed by Sample A subjects in 1980. Recent modifications (McCrae and Costa, 1987) have added two new scales to measure the domains of Agreeableness (A) and Conscientiousness (C). Self-reports on 10- and 14-item preliminary forms of the A and C scales were obtained by mail administration in 1983 from a subset of 447 Sample A subjects . . . The published version of the NEO-PI was administered by mail to Samples A and B, in 1986. This version differs from the earlier form in minor modifications, in the wording of a few questions and in the addition of eight Agreeableness and four Conscientiousness items. . . . An observer-rating version of the NEO-PI, Form-R, parallels the self-report version except that items are phrased in the third person . . . Spouse ratings on the three-domain NEO Inventory were collected from about half of the Sample A subjects in 1980 (McCrae, 1982). In 1986, the full NEO-PI, Form R was administered to spouses.

The NEO-PI, Form-R is the spouse-rating version of the NEO Personality Inventory. In summary, Sample A participants' personality traits were assessed over a six-year period (in 1980 and in 1986). They completed self-reports in 1980 using the NEO Inventory to measure Neuroticism, Extraversion and Openness to Experience. Agreeableness and Conscientiousness were measured using two new scales in 1983. They completed self-reports again in 1986; these were done using a later version of the inventory, called the NEO-PI which measured all five traits. Spouse ratings were done in 1980 on the three-domain NEO by about half of Sample A. Spouses again rated their partner's traits in 1986 using full NEO-PI, Form R.

Results

1. Stability and Change in Mean Levels
. . . In the present study, conventional cross-sectional and longitudinal analyses are supplemented with cross- and time-sequential analyses to facilitate inferences about age changes in personality . . .

The results are presented in two sections; one for mean levels and one for individual differences in personality stability. For simplicity, we will focus only on longitudinal analyses for both of these sections.

Repeated Measures Analyses
. . . The usual alternative to the cross-sectional study is the longitudinal design, in which the same individuals are retested some years later . . . Being retested itself, however, can influence scores on the second administration . . . generally labelled a *practice* effect . . . In addition, changes in the variables over the retest period may be due to social changes that have nothing to do with universal maturational processes. Such effects are referred to as *secular* or *period* effects . . . Self-report data from 398 subjects were analyzed for N, E and O scales, and data from 360 subjects were analyzed for the short A and C scales.

'Repeated measures' is the type of design where the same participants are used in each condition of the study. So, in the longitudinal design, the same people complete the personality inventory in both 1980 and 1986. Costa and McCrae here acknowledge the limitations of such a design, such as practice effects.

Results . . . show declines over the retest interval for Anxiety, Impulsiveness and total Neuroticism, an increase in Warmth but a decline in Activity, and an increase in Fantasy but a decline in openness to Actions. Both Agreeableness and Conscientiousness declined . . . Repeated measures analyses were also possible for spouse ratings . . . Results showed significant increases in Hostility, Self-Consciousness, Impulsiveness, Vulnerability, total Neuroticism, Warmth, and openness to Fantasy and Values as well as declines in Activity, Positive Emotions, and openness to Actions. There were no significant changes in total Extraversion or Openness . . .

Interpretations and Implications
. . . the data strongly support the stability position. Most of the effects seen account for less than 1% of variance. Such small effects may be due to subtle influences of changes in wording or test format . . . A conservative interpretation . . . therefore, would be that if there are

> maturational changes in personality, they are likely to account for a change of less than one standard deviation during the full course of adult life . . .

These are the findings for the longitudinal study. They state the findings in terms of the Big Five traits and their subordinate traits (e.g. Anxiety and Impulsiveness are subordinate traits of Neuroticism. Warmth and Activity are subordinate traits of Extraversion; see Boxes 8.1 and 8.3). They found that some traits declined while others increased. For the self-reports, they found increases in Warmth (E) (letters in brackets signify the superordinate trait, such as Extraversion) and Fantasy (O) but declines in Anxiety (N), Impulsiveness (N), total Neuroticism, Activity (E), openness to Actions (O), Conscientiousness and Agreeableness. For spouse ratings, they found increases in Hostility (N), Self-Consciousness (N), Impulsiveness (N), Vulnerability (N), total Neuroticism, Warmth (E), and openness to Fantasy (O) and Values (O) as well as declines in Activity (E), Positive Emotions (E), and openness to Actions (O). They found no changes in total Extraversion or Openness. The results for mean levels indicate that there are some increases or decreases in some traits over the six-year period. However, these are only small changes. It thus appears that traits are stable over time.

2. Stability of Individual Differences

The failure to find changes in the average level of personality traits due to aging, does not necessarily imply that individuals have remained unchanged in personality. It would be theoretically possible for all to have undergone radical changes in every aspect of personality, so long as the increases of some individuals were balanced by the decreases of others. To assess the stability of individual differences, retest correlations are necessary, and only data from Sample A can be used.

Retest Stability in Self-Reports

. . . retest correlations for the N, E, and O domains over a 6-year interval and for A and C domains over a 3-year interval [are calculated] . . . In general, it appears that personality is about equally stable for men and women over age 30 and for younger and older adults . . . These results are expectable in the cases of Neuroticism and Extraversion, which have frequently been shown to have high levels of stability in adulthood. Openness to Experience, however, has rarely been studied longitudinally; the retest coefficients seen in that domain are therefore particularly informative and suggest that Openness is as stable as Neuroticism and Extraversion . . . In the case of Conscientiousness, the 3-year stability seems to be comparable with the 6-year stability of the N, E, and O domains, despite the brevity of the scale. The A scale, however, shows a distinctly lower stability coefficient . . . As with mean levels, conclusions regarding the stability of Agreeableness and Conscientiousness must be tentative, pending data over a longer interval with the full scales. At a minimum, however, it appears that both these domains show considerable stability in the rank of ordering of individuals.

Retest Stability of Spouse Ratings
. . . spouse ratings provide an alternative to self-reports for estimating the stability of personality traits . . . stability coefficients for spouse ratings of traits in N,E, and O domains [show] impressive levels of stability for both men and women over a 6-year interval.

Retest stability (retest correlations) is the correlation between the personality inventory ratings at time one (i.e. 1980) and time two (i.e. 1986).

Discussion

In contrast to the analyses of mean level changes, where a variety of significant but small and conflicting findings lent only indirect support to the premise that personality shows little change in average level attribut-able to maturation, the analyses of retest stability provided unequivocal evidence for the stability of individual differences. All of the five major domains of normal personality showed stability in self-reports of men and women across the adult age range; spouse ratings confirmed this stability for Neuroticism, Extraversion, and Openness . . . Several points remain for future research. [such as] Some of the conflicting findings on mean level changes may be due to differences in the form of the test, and a replica-tion using the published version of the test on both occasions would be desirable . . .

It appears from the data of many longitudinal studies that aging itself has little effect on personality. This is true despite the fact that the normal course of aging includes disease, bereavement, divorce, unemployment, and many other significant events for substantial portions of the popula-tion. One important direction for future research lies in tracing the limits of the generalization of stability for specific groups, especially including individuals with psychiatric or neuropsychological impairments. The use of observer ratings may be particularly important in these cases, where the validity of self-reports may be questionable. Data from the present study suggest that raters (at least spouses) may be expected to show high levels of stability in normal populations. Marked changes would probably be meaningful as indications of real change in patient groups.

The findings of this study indicate that, for mean levels of traits, there are some small changes in personality during adulthood. However, the results for individual differences show that personality is stable during adulthood for all five traits. Furthermore, this was confirmed for Neuroticism, Extraversion and Openness to Experience by the spouse ratings. The researchers discuss some limitations of their study, which may have affected their findings. For example, it would be advantageous to use the NEO-PI for both of 1980 and 1986, instead of separate A and C scales in 1983 (this was not possible at the time). It is possible that changes in trait levels were a product of differences between these methods rather than real changes.

Summary of Costa and McCrae (1988)

Costa and McCrae investigated one of the fundamental questions in personality: whether our personality changes during adulthood or whether it stays the same (is stable). They focused on the 'Big Five' traits of personality and used versions of the NEO Inventory (a questionnaire) to measure these. They used a large sample of men and women and self-reports, as well as spouse ratings. People's personalities were assessed over six years, using longitudinal and cross-sectional methods as well as sequential methods. They looked at two aspects of personality change: the mean levels of traits in a population and individual's trait levels. They found some small changes in mean levels of traits across the six-year period, but these were small. Overall they found that personality is largely stable during adulthood.

Costa and McCrae have continued to study personality and, they propose that an individual's personality at 30 years old is a good indication of their personality at 80 years old. However, other researchers argue that personality is not so stable. For example, Ardelt (2000) states that such factors as the length of time between the two personality assessments, and age at the time of the first assessment, affect how stable personality appears to be. Personality is found to be less stable when the interval between assessments is of twenty years or more, and personality is less stable if the person is under 30 years old or over 50 years old at the first assessment. It also appears that personality appears to be stable using the NEO inventories, but is less stable when using other questionnaires which are not based on the Big Five traits.

Summary of individual differences

The psychology of individual differences is still a relatively new area of psychology. It looks at how individual people differ in their own right rather than aiming to determine general laws of human behaviour. However, as people are complex, there are many theories and there is much evidence as to what the

Box 8.5 Research: other research in individual differences

Darviri and Woods (2006): How does personality relate to time off work?
Many people take days off work even though they are not sick. Does their personality influence whether they are likely to take days off work? Sevasti Darviri and Stephen Woods questioned whether an individual's personality relates to them unofficially taking time off, and if so, in what way. They examined this issue using the 'Big Five' personality traits of Neuroticism, Extraversion, Openness to Experience, Agreeableness and Conscientiousness. Darviri and Woods distinguished between absence from work due to a person's choice (e.g. they would rather meet their friends) or due to events around them which are outside of their control (e.g. they need to look after a sick child). They predicted that the Big Five personality traits would relate to absenteeism but only for when a person is absent due to their choice. For instance, a highly extravert person who is sociable and gregarious may be more likely to take time off work to do a leisure activity (e.g. meet friends) than someone who is low on extraversion.

They asked 128 office-based workers in the Greek construction industry to complete a questionnaire which assessed the Big Five personality traits. The workers then rated how likely they were to take time off work in the future for a variety of reasons. The reasons were either related to being absent due to events outside of their control (e.g. time off for childcare) or to being absent by choice (e.g. just not feeling like coming into work). They found that three of the Big Five traits were correlated to future intention to take time off work but only for reasons of choice. Specifically, they found that the higher a person scored on Extraversion and Openness to Experience, and the less they scored on Agreeableness, the more likely they were to take unofficial time off in the future. It appears that personality does influence whether a person will take days off work when it is for reasons within their own control.

Van Coillie, Van Mechelen and Ceulemans (2006): Individual differences in anger.
Not all people show the same behaviour when they are angry with someone. Van Coillie, Van Mechelen and Ceulemans explored these individual differences in people's anger-related behaviour. They asked 364 participants to recall nine instances where they had been angry with someone. They had to write the instances down and then read them again in order to recreate being back in that situation. They then indicated how much they wanted to display, and did actually show, eight anger behaviours. These included physical aggression (e.g. hitting someone, throwing things), anger towards yourself (e.g. starting to drink) or relaxing yourself (e.g. listening to music, running). Participants also completed three personality questionnaires which measured the Big Five personality traits, their self-expression and control of anger and their disposition to experience anger.

They found that there are individual differences in anger-related behaviours; not everyone, if angry, responds in the same way. These individual differences mainly arise in three areas: people differ in their levels of external physical and verbal aggression, in how they reduce the tension of being angry (e.g. by letting the feeling fade) and in how they talk about and show they are moved (e.g. by crying or talking about it).

principal aspects of psychological differences are. It covers a large array of topics, such as how people differ in personality and intelligence. Box 8.5 summarizes some other research in this area. Research in this area has practical applications. For example, personality tests can be used to diagnose mental illness or to match people to suitable occupations. It is also now recognized that personality can predict a wide range of behavioural and social outcomes. For example, personality assessments can predict work performance and personality factors are strongly associated with mental health problems (e.g. depression, substance abuse).

9 Clinical psychology

This chapter describes clinical psychology and examines one research paper in depth.

- The area: clinical psychology focuses on the assessment and treatment of mental disorders.
- The research: how long do the benefits of cognitive-behavioural therapy last for schizophrenia?

What is clinical psychology?

Clinical psychology is concerned with mental disorders (see Box 9.1). It is the branch of psychology that assesses, diagnoses and treats people who are suffering from mental disorders. It also researches into the causes of, treatments and prevention for, such disorders. Clinical psychologists work with people

---

 Box 9.1 Details: what are mental disorders?

Mental disorders are also known as mental illness or psychological disorders (e.g. depression, anxiety disorders, eating disorders). Mental disorders are where a person's psychological functioning (their thinking, emotion and/or behaviour) departs from what is considered to be normal. The Diagnostic and Statistical Manual of Mental Disorder (DSM) (see Box 9.2) defines mental disorder as a clinically significant problem associated with distress, a loss of functioning, a significantly increased risk of suffering or loss of freedom. You may also come across the term 'abnormal psychology' which is the scientific study of psychopathology.

suffering from such problems as anxiety, depression, eating disorders, relationship problems and schizophrenia, amongst others. Clinical psychologists assess clients using psychometric tests, interviews and direct observation. Clinical psychologists typically do not prescribe psychiatric drugs. Clinical psychology differs from counselling in that clinical psychologists treat more severe disorders, such as phobias and schizophrenia, whereas counselling psychologists work with patients suffering from everyday worries, such as marriage and family problems.

Some consider 1896 to be the 'official' year that clinical psychology was established. In this year, the American psychologist Lightner Witmer (1867–1956) first set up a psychology clinic to treat school children suffering from retardation (he introduced the term 'clinical psychology' in 1907). Freud also used the word 'psychoanalysis' for first time in 1896. However, people have always been aware of mental illness. The Ebers Papyrus (circa 1600 BC), one of the earliest known medical documents, mentions mental illness. What society and the medical profession have viewed to be mental illness has changed over time. For example, in the early 1800s 'madness' included sexual promiscuity and alcoholism. Explanations for mental illness have included demonic or divine possession, bad living, punishment for sins, having a displaced womb and so on.

Treatments for mental illness has also changed over time. For example, it was thought people could be treated by driving evil spirits out of the body. Phillipe Pinel (1745–1826) reformed the treatment of the mentally ill in 1798 by removing shackles from severely mentally disturbed women at La Salpetrière, a Paris asylum. This more humanitarian treatment was based on the belief that mental illness is a disease that must be understood and treated using scientific methods. Emil Kraepelin (1855–1925) began the practice of diagnosing and classifying mental disorders in the same way as physical disorders (see Box 9.2). By the 1840s, psychiatry had become a medical specialism in the United Kingdom. In the 1960s/1970s, an antipsychiatry movement developed which objected to the increasing use of drug treatments, **electro-convulsive therapy, lobotomies** and so on. For example, Thomas Szasz (1960) argued that mental illnesses are really 'problems of living' and that labelling a person as mentally ill has adverse effects (for example, all of the person's actions being interpreted according to their illness, even when their actions are normal). Knowledge about the causes of mental illnesses has advanced and by the mid-1970s there was increased understanding about the biological causes of such illnesses. Since the 1970s, clinical psychology has been a subdiscipline in its own right and psychology has established itself as an authority dealing with behavioural and psychological problems.

Clinical psychology not only offers help for mental disorders but also conducts research into such issues as the causes of illnesses or the best treatment

Box 9.2 Methods: diagnosing mental disorders

Being able to diagnose a mental disorder depends on having a set of classifying symptoms for that disorder. Several classification systems have been set up, but the most used is the Diagnostic and Statistical Manual of Mental Disorders (known as DSM). It was first published in 1952 by the American Psychiatric Association. The latest version to date is DSM-IV-TR (which means fourth edition, text revision), which is a revision of DMS-IV (APA, 1994). Clinical psychologists and other mental health professionals use this manual as a reference for all types of mental disorder. DSM-IV lists and describes over 200 diagnostic categories of mental disorder and gives specific criteria used to diagnose any one illness. These criteria specify what symptoms must be present, and for how long, in order to diagnose a disorder (inclusion criteria) and specifies symptoms that must not be present (exclusion criteria). A patient is evaluated on five axes (scales) which cover: the actual syndrome diagnosed (e.g. paranoid schizophrenia); any additional problems (e.g. personality disorders); physical problems; any stressful events that may be relevant (e.g. death of a loved one); and global assessment of functioning (which rates the person's social, occupational and psychological functioning for the present and past year).

for them. In this chapter, we focus on a piece of research which investigates the effectiveness of one specific treatment for the psychological disorder of schizophrenia.

Research paper

Mike Startup, Mike Jackson, Keith Evans and Sue Bendix researched how one type of therapy helps people suffering from schizophrenia. They published their findings in the *Psychological Medicine* journal in 2005. In some previous research (Startup *et al.*, 2004) they had found that a form of therapy, called cognitive behaviour therapy (in addition to the usual treatment) had helped to alleviate some symptoms of schizophrenia more than just the usual treatment alone. This benefit had lasted for one year. In the Startup *et al.* (2005) research described in this chapter, they examined if this benefit had lasted two years and also assessed its financial implications. Before turning to the research paper, we will review what schizophrenia and cognitive behaviour therapy are.

Background: schizophrenia and cognitive behaviour therapy

Schizophrenia is a severe **psychotic** disorder in which the person experiences disturbances in thinking, attention, motivation and emotion, and disrupted relationships. It is not correct that a person with schizophrenia has a **split personality** or **multiple personalities**. This disorder was first described by Emil Kraepelin in 1883. Eugen Bleuler (1857–1939) originated the name 'schizophrenia' in 1911, using the Greek *schizo* meaning split and *phren* meaning mind. Schizophrenia tends to first appear in adolescence or early adulthood, with 1 in 100 people having the disorder.

Psychologists describe the symptoms of schizophrenia as positive or negative (see Box 9.3). Positive (psychotic) symptoms are those which add on to normal thought patterns and experience. Such symptoms include delusions, hallucinations and thought disorder. Delusions are strange, unjustifiable beliefs, such as the person's belief that someone is trying to kill him/her. Hallucinations are strange perceptual experiences, such as hearing voices or seeing auras around people. Thought disorder is odd, illogical reasoning, such as feeling that thoughts have been inserted into your mind. In contrast, negative symptoms are a reduction of normal activity. These include, for example, flattened affect, reduced motor activity, alogia and avolition. Flattened affect (emotion) is a reduced range and intensity of emotions (e.g. less eye contact, an immobile face). Reduced motor activity is a lack of spontaneous movement, such as remaining still for hours (catatonia). Alogia is a reduced fluency of speech and avolition is difficulty in initiating things (e.g. having no motivation to eat or dress). Schizophrenia is sometimes classed into two types: type I is where the person has mostly positive symptoms, whereas type II is where the person has mostly negative symptoms. DSM-IV (see Box 9.4) also lists five subtypes of schizophrenia.

Schizophrenia can be treated with drugs. Antipsychotic drugs reduce psychotic symptoms (positive ones) but do not affect negative symptoms. An alternative to drugs is 'talking therapies', which are psychological therapies. One example is cognitive behaviour therapy (CBT). CBT is a combination of cognitive psychology and behavioural therapy. Behavioural therapy is where mental disorder is treated by the person unlearning maladjusted behaviours and relearning better adjusted ones. CBT aims to help people by primarily altering the way they think, which in turn makes them feel and behave differently; it helps people learn more adaptive ways of thinking as well as behaving.

CBT is usually done in a one-to-one session between the client and therapist, but it can also be done in groups. Clients attend one session a week, with each session lasting about an hour. During this time, the client and therapist work together to understand what the problems are and to develop a new way of tackling them. CBT teaches the client a set of coping skills which they can

Box 9.3 Methods: diagnosing schizophrenia

Below is a summary of the DSM-IV (APA, 1994) criteria for a diagnosis of schizophrenia.

a) Two (or more) of the following symptoms must be shown, each for a significant amount of time during a one-month period. Only one of these symptoms is needed if delusions are bizarre or hallucinations consist of a voice keeping up a running commentary on the person's behaviour or thoughts, or two or more voices conversing with each other.

- Delusions. These are false beliefs which a person holds in spite of evidence to the contrary. For example, delusions of grandeur are when the person believes that they are very special or have special powers or abilities, such as thinking they are the king.
- Hallucinations. These can be visual, auditory, tactile, **olfactory** or **gustatory** experiences (e.g. tasting things that are not present).
- Disorganized speech. This is where the person's speech frequently changes tack or is incoherent (also called 'word salads').
- Grossly disorganized or catatonic behaviour. This is where the person shows stupour or inactivity, **mania** and rigidity or extreme flexibility of the limbs.
- Negative symptoms. These are a lack of important abilities, such as having low energy (sitting around and sleeping much more than normal) or social isolation where the person spends most of the day alone or only with close family.
- Cognitive symptoms. These refer to difficulties with concentration and memory.

b) Social/occupational dysfunction. This specifies that, for a significant amount of time since the symptoms began, one/more aspects of functioning (e.g. work, relationships, self-care) have been distinctly below the level of functioning prior to the onset.

c) Duration. Continuous signs of the disturbance have persisted for at least six-months. In this six-month period, there must have been at least one month of symptoms that meet Criterion a.

d) Schizoaffective and mood disorder exclusion. These disorders have been ruled out because there has been no major depressive, **manic** or mood episodes when the schizophrenic symptoms are active.

e) Substance/general medical condition exclusion. This rules out the possibility that the symptoms are due to the effects of a substance (e.g. a drug of abuse or a medication) or a general medical condition.

f) Relationship to a pervasive developmental disorder. If there is a history of autistic or another developmental disorder, the additional diagnosis of schizophrenia is made only if prominent delusions or hallucinations have also been present for at least one month.

Box 9.4 Details: subtypes of schizophrenia

DSM-IV lists five subtypes which are:

- Disorganized schizophrenia. This subtype involves great disorganization, such as delusions, hallucinations, incoherent thought and speech.
- Catatonic schizophrenia. Mainly immobility for hours at a time alternating with frenzied behaviour.
- Paranoid schizophrenia. Involves mostly complex delusions.
- Undifferentiated schizophrenia. This is a broad category which includes patients who do not clearly belong in the other subtypes.
- Residual schizophrenia. This includes patients who gradually develop only mild symptoms, such as social withdrawal.

apply whenever they need to. For example, a person suffering from anxiety may learn that avoiding situations actually increases their fears, so confronting these gradually helps the person gain confidence in their own ability to cope. There is much evidence that CBT is an effective treatment for such disorders as depression, anxiety, phobias and sleep problems, amongst others. It is currently a very popular therapy. However, it can be less effective for other disorders (e.g. alcohol dependency). Most studies into its effectiveness have focused on its short-term effects and relatively little is known about the long-term effects of CBT.

The paper

Startup, M., Jackson, M.C., Evans, K.E. and Bendix, S. (2005) North Wales randomized controlled trial of cognitive behaviour therapy for acute schizophrenia spectrum disorders: two-year follow-up and economic evaluation. *Psychological Medicine*, 35: 1307–16.

Abstract

Background: There is good evidence now that cognitive behaviour therapy (CBT) is effective in the treatment of people suffering from schizophrenia. There is also some evidence that the benefits of CBT persist after the end of treatment and that the direct costs of providing CBT, as an adjunct to standard care, are no higher than the direct costs of standard care alone. The aims of the present study were to discover if the benefits of CBT for acute schizophrenia which were found one year after index admission persist for another year, and to evaluate the comparative costs of providing CBT.

Method: Consecutive admissions meeting criteria were recruited. After screening, 43 were assigned at random to a treatment as usual (TAU) control group and 47 were assigned to TAU plus CBT. Patients (73% of original) were rated on symptoms and social functioning two years after index admission. An evaluation of the direct costs of services was also complete.

Results: The CBT group had maintained its advantage over the TAU group on negative symptoms and social functioning, but had lost the advantage it previously enjoyed in positive symptoms. The difference between the groups, in total direct costs over the two years, was not statistically significant despite the cost of providing CBT.

Conclusions: Some of the benefits of CBT for patients suffering acute psychotic episodes persist for two years. After the end of the regular treatment, CBT should probably be targeted on the appearance of early signs of relapse to forestall the re-emergence of positive symptoms.

The abstract summarizes what is already known from previous research and describes the aims, results and conclusions of this research. Social functioning is the ability to interact normally with others and to form healthy social relationships. See Chapter 2 for an explanation of 'statistically significant'. A person with schizophrenia does not show symptoms all of the time; a psychotic episode is a period when the person does show the symptoms (e.g. experiencing hallucinations and delusions). 'Acute' means that the disorder or episode is of a short time, progresses rapidly and needs care urgently.

Introduction

There is good evidence now that cognitive behaviour therapy (CBT) is effective, as an adjunct to standard care, in the treatment of people suffering from schizophrenia (Gould *et al.*, 2001; Pilling *et al.*, 2002) . . . Several more recent trials have added to this evidence for the efficacy of CBT (Gaudiano, 2005). In one trial, which is the focus of the present study, Startup *et al.* (2004) compared the effects of CBT, as an addition to treatment as usual (TAU), with TAU alone for patients who had recently been admitted to a psychiatric hospital as a result of suffering an acute psychotic episode. The results showed significant advantages for the CBT group by 12 months after baseline on positive and negative symptoms and social functioning . . .

The baseline is the first assessment of the patient on admission.

There is also some evidence that the effects of CBT for schizophrenia are durable. In their review, Gould *et al.* (2001) found that patients treated with CBT continued to improve after the end of treatment . . . for follow-ups ranging from 9 to 18 months. Since that review was completed, the results of four follow-ups of 18 months or longer have been published [For example] Tarrier *et al.* (2000), in a follow-up of their comparison of CBT, supportive counselling and routine care for persistent symptoms in chronic schizophrenia, found that the gains the CBT group had made in their positive and negative symptoms during the course of treatment declined over the next 2 years, and the survival times to relapse did not differ significantly between the three groups. Although the results for CBT were significantly better than those for routine care, the results for supportive counselling were better than those for CBT at two years even though the counselling intervention was designed as a **placebo** control . . . Outcomes at 18 months have also been reported recently by Tarrier *et al.* (2004). During their treatment phase, schizophrenic inpatients who were suffering either their first or their second acute psychotic episode were offered either CBT, supportive counselling or TAU alone. It was found that the treated groups had significantly improved positive, negative and general symptoms at 18 months, compared with TAU, but the CBT and counselling groups did not differ from each other.

'Chronic' is when a disorder is of indefinite duration, and shows virtually no change over time. A placebo can be used as a control group; groups of patients are compared, one group receives the treatment being investigated and one group receives a placebo.

These recent results are somewhat inconsistent but they suggest that the benefits of CBT for negative symptoms tend to persist but, the benefits for positive symptoms and social functioning, are variable in the long-term. The main aim of the present study was to add to the evidence on the durability of the effects of CBT by reporting the results of a randomized controlled trial of CBT for acute schizophrenia spectrum disorders two years after index admission to hospital. It is not certain that providing CBT for psychotic patients as an addition to routine care is more expensive than routine care alone since it might be that the additional costs of providing CBT are offset by savings in other aspects of service provision, such as hospital admissions and crisis interventions . . . Only two economic evaluations of CBT for psychosis appear to have been published to date . . . there was no evidence in either of these evaluations that providing CBT to patients with schizophrenia, in addition to their routine care is more expensive that routine care alone. A second aim of the present study was to test whether the same conclusion holds when CBT is provided to inpatients suffering acute psychotic episodes.

The introduction first describes the results of previous research. The previous evidence suggests that CBT, in addition to standard care, does help people with schizophrenia, and this benefit can last for up to one year or more. However, the evidence is inconsistent. It appears that, in the long-term, CBT has benefits for negative symptoms, whereas the benefits for positive symptoms and social functioning vary. This study aims to assess the effects of CBT on the symptoms of schizophrenia at two years after first being admitted. This research is following-up patients involved in the Startup *et al.* (2004) investigation, when the patients were assessed at one year. Here they are assessed again at two years. 'Randomized' means that participants were randomly allocated to the treatment groups. 'Schizophrenia spectrum disorders' are disorders which have some of the same symptoms as schizophrenia, such as **schizoaffective disorder**. The researchers do also discuss the relative cost of providing CBT on top of routine care but for simplicity in this chapter, we will concentrate on the findings of providing CBT and not on the cost.

Method

The methods of the acute phase of this trial and their rationale are presented in full by Startup *et al.* (2004) and only a summary is provided below. The design of this follow-up was a naturalistic study of the trial participants who were available for assessment 24 months after baseline assessment.

See Table 2.3 (p. 20) for an explanation of a naturalistic study.

Participants
Consecutive admissions to three acute psychiatric hospitals were considered eligible for inclusion if they were aged between 18 and 65 years, had received a clinical diagnosis of a schizophrenia spectrum disorder, were suffering an acute psychotic episode and showed no evidence of organic mental disorder. Those who accepted the invitation to participate in the research were then included provided their diagnoses could be confirmed according to DSM-IV criteria (APA, 1994), their IQs were at least 80, they had not been dependent on alcohol or illicit drugs during the previous year, and no more than 28 days had passed since they had been admitted. Ninety patients met these criteria, 43 of whom were assigned at random to a treatment as usual (TAU) control group and 47 were assigned to TAU plus CBT.

These are the criteria used to select participants for the first phase which is presented in the 2004 study. 'Organic mental disorder' is a disorder which is associated with brain damage, such as Alzheimer's disease. The patients were assigned at random to the TAU group or to the CBT plus TAU group by tossing a coin in front of an assessor.

> *Treatment conditions*
> TAU, in the three participating Trusts of the UK National Health Service (NHS), consists of pharmacotherapy, nursing care during hospitalization and community care after discharge . . . CBT, provided as an addition to TAU . . . [was] a highly individualized, needs-based form of CBT for psychotic disorders . . . Appointments for treatment were provided at weekly intervals, where possible, and the length of each appointment was adjusted flexibly according to the patients' requirements. Therapy began immediately after baseline assessment and continued, without interruption, following discharge . . . CBT was provided by three clinical psychologists. Two of them were employed as specialists in serious mental illness and conducted CBT for schizophrenia on a routine basis and the third had recently undertaken a one-year specialist training in CBT for psychotic disorders.

'Pharmacotherapy' is treatment of disease and mental disorder with drugs. The CBT patients had up to a maximum of 25 sessions. Each appointment length was 90 minutes, at most.

> *Clinical measures*
> At baseline assessment and at 6, 12 and 24 months after baseline, patients were rated, following structured interviews by trained assessors, on the Scale for the Assessment of Positive Symptoms (SAPS; Andreason, 1984) and the Scale for the Assessment of Negative Symptoms (SANS: Andreason, 1989). Global ratings for hallucinations and delusions were summed to form a score for psychotic symptoms and global ratings for all the SANS items were summed to form a score for negative symptoms. Following structured interviews with 'best informants', the patients were rated by the interviewers on the Social Functioning Scale (SFS; Birchwood *et al.*, 1990) and, at the end of this interview, the patients were rated by both interviewer and informant independently on the Global Assessment of Functioning (GAF; APA, 1994). All interviews referred to the preceding month . . . Since these levels of agreement were excellent, averages of the two sets of ratings were used in all subsequent analyses involving the GAF . . .

Data analyses

... Scores on the main outcome variables, the psychotic subscale of the SAPS, the SANS total, the SFS, and the GAF for baseline and the three follow-up assessments were analysed ... Results were also analysed for individual outcome in terms of reliable and clinically significant change. The GAF was chosen as the outcome variable for this analysis since it provides a valid summary of both symptoms and social functioning ...

See Table 2.1 (p. 18) for a description of a structured interview. Four scales were used to assess the patient's symptoms and functioning. The SAPS assessed their positive symptoms, the SANS gauged their negative symptoms, the SFS assessed their social functioning and the GAF measured their overall psychological, occupational and social functioning. Best informants are described in Startup *et al.* (2004) as qualified mental health professionals who manage the patient's care. The treatment group is an independent variable (CBT plus TAU or TAU). The dependent variables are the scores on the four assessment scales (SAPS, SANS, SFS and GAF). Patients were assessed at baseline (admission), at six months, and at one year (in the Startup *et al.* 2004 research paper). In this paper (2005), the same patients were assessed at two years after baseline. The data were analysed for (a) differences between CBT and TAU groups on the four scales and (b) how individuals changed on the GAF scale.

Results

Patient attrition

Although every effort was made to follow-up all patients, interviews could not be conducted with 30 patients at two years for the following reasons: 12 refused, 12 had moved away, two were detained in prison, one was too dangerous, one had withdrawn from the research, and two had committed suicide. Informants were unable to provide information on 24 patients for the following reasons: 12 had moved away, seven were refusing to see the informant, two were in prison, one had withdrawn from the research and two had committed suicide. The numbers in each group who were available for follow-up assessment did not differ significantly between the two groups. Differences at baseline between those who were available for follow-up and those who were not were analysed ... None of the results was significant at this level [$p < 0.01$].

Attrition is the loss of patients from the research for various reasons. Here, the researchers describe why some patients were unavailable. It is important that these numbers do not differ as this could affect the analysis and results. Likewise, it is important that the remaining patients do not differ in their first baseline assessment.

Symptoms and social functioning

The crucial interactions between group and assessment occasion for the GAF . . . SAPS positive symptoms . . . SANS negative symptoms . . . and the SFS . . . were all significant . . . All of the differences between groups were in favour of the CBT group, but only differences in negative symptoms and social functioning were significant . . . It can be seen that the positive symptoms of the CBT group have increased since the one-year follow-up and that this group no longer enjoys the advantage it once had, but the difference between groups in negative symptoms has continued to widen. The difference between groups in social functioning has remained roughly constant, although both have deteriorated slightly in this respect. The GAF summarizes these changes by showing a narrowing gap between groups.

Results on the GAF were analysed for individual outcome . . . It can be seen that a larger proportion of patients in the CBT group showed reliable and clinically significant improvement and a larger proportion of patients in the TAU group showed reliable deterioration . . .

Medication and admissions to hospital

Mean dosages of antipsychotic medication during the four weeks preceding each assessment . . . are shown . . . The non-significant differences between groups at the first two follow-ups have been reported by Startup *et al.* (2004). At two-year follow-up dosages for the CBT group . . . and the TAU group . . . did not differ significantly . . ..the two groups did not differ significantly on number of days in hospital . . . nor on number of readmissions . . . Times until first readmission to hospital during the two-year follow-up period were also analysed . . . Although the survival time for the CBT group . . . was longer than that for the TAU group . . . the proportion of the CBT group that were readmitted at least once was smaller . . . than the proportion of the TAU group . . .

The findings are that, at two years after admission, there are statistically significant differences between the treatment groups (CBT and TAU) on all four scales. It was found that the CBT group were better than the TAU group for negative symptoms and for social functioning. The CBT group were better than the TAU group for negative symptoms, and this gap was still getting wider. For social functioning, the difference between the groups was still about the same. However, this difference was not found for positive symptoms. The CBT group's positive symptoms had got worse. They also found that more patients in the CBT group had improved, while more patients in the TAU group had worsened. As there was no difference in medication between the groups, this cannot be the reason for any difference in their symptoms and/or functioning.

Discussion

The results for symptoms and social functioning at two-year follow-up provided a mixed picture. The difference between groups in negative symptoms was significant, as it had been one year earlier; the CBT group had continued to improve while the TAU group had stayed the same. This is similar to the result obtained . . . at two-year follow-up by Tarrier *et al.* (2000) for their CBT group, whose negative symptoms remained stable over the second year of follow-up. Both groups in the present study had deteriorated slightly in social functioning over the previous year but the difference between groups remained significant at two years. This is comparable to the result for global functioning that Haddock *et al.* (2003) reported at 18-month follow-up. However, the advantage in delusions and hallucinations that the CBT group had enjoyed in the present study at one year had been lost; their positive symptoms had increased since one-year follow-up and appeared to be converging with the slightly improving positive symptoms of the control group. A similar result was obtained at two-year follow-up by Tarrier *et al.* (2000) for their CBT group except that, in their case, positive symptoms began to deteriorate before 12-month follow-up. These results suggest that, in order to prevent recurrence of positive symptoms, 'booster' sessions of CBT should be offered at intervals following termination of regular treatment.

The evidence for a decline in functioning was confirmed by the analysis of individual outcomes. At two years, only 50% of the CBT group still showed reliable and clinically significant change (compared to baseline) whereas 60% had met these criteria at one-year follow-up. However, the decline in the TAU group was even greater, down from 40% to 25%, and the differences between groups in categorical outcome were still significant. These differences cannot be explained by differences in medication as the median dose for the two groups . . . was the same.

On average, the CBT group compared to the TAU group had fewer admissions to hospital, spent fewer days in hospital over the two years, and survived longer outside hospital, but none of these differences was significant. This is similar to comparable results for relapses reported by Tarrier *et al.* (2002) and Haddock *et al.* (2003) in which large differences in group means were nevertheless non-significant because of large amounts of variability within groups. Thus, it may be that CBT is effective in reducing hospitalization but much larger samples will be required to demonstrate this. Nevertheless, the fact that 61% of the CBT group were readmitted to hospital at least once (70% of the TAU group) shows that CBT was not effective in maintaining patients in the community once treatment was terminated, despite the large improvements in symptoms and social functioning that were obtained during treatment (Startup *et al.*

2004). This finding suggests that warning signs of relapse should be monitored continuously and CBT should be targeted when they appear. Such an approach to relapse prevention has been found to be effective with patients who are prone to relapse (Gumley *et al.* 2003) . . . the difference between groups in hospital costs was not statistically significant, nor was the difference in total direct costs over the two years but, equally, there was no evidence that providing CBT led to greater direct costs . . . Since this research involved patients, settings, therapists and conditions of therapy that are broadly representative of routine clinical practice (Startup *et al.* 2004), in the United Kingdom at least, the average costs per patient should also be representative of the average costs of providing the same treatment in typical settings elsewhere.

One of the limitations of this research was . . . that a large proportion (33%) of participants were unavailable for follow-up interviews. However . . . the proportions who were unavailable did not differ between groups, and those who were unavailable did not differ from those who were available on any measure at baseline. Therefore, we think it unlikely that the attrition rate has biased the results . . .

In conclusion, providing CBT for patients with schizophrenia who have been admitted to hospital as a result of an acute psychotic episode is likely to be no more expensive than routine care, but should secure for those patients advantages in terms of negative symptoms and social functioning which persist for at least two years.

This discussion section summarizes the findings and then discusses whether these findings support previous research, any limitations and suggestions for future research. Here we can see one benefit of doing research; a possible intervention treatment (booster session) is suggested to help stave off the positive symptoms. They found no difference in cost for providing CBT in addition to the standard care (TAU) compared to providing standard care alone.

Summary of Startup *et al.* (2005)

Mike Startup and colleagues conducted their research to examine if a psychological therapy, CBT, helps people suffering from schizophrenia more than the standard treatment and whether the benefits continue two years later. Their research (2005) followed up previous research done in 2004 (Startup *et al.*, 2004). In the 2004 study, they had recruited patients with schizophrenia who had been admitted to hospital with an acute psychotic episode. Forty-three patients were given the standard care (treatment as usual; which included antipsychotic medicine and nursing care). Forty-seven patients were given additional sessions of CBT provided by clinical psychologists. The patients were assessed at the time of admission (baseline), and again at six months and at one year. They found that patients who had had the additional CBT sessions had fewer negative and positive symptoms, and better social functioning at one year than those who had only standard treatment. Also, the CBT patients showed more improvement than the standard treatment group.

In 2005, they reassessed 73 per cent of these patients at two years after their baseline assessment. They found that the CBT patients were still better on negative symptoms and social functioning than the standard treatment patients. However, this was not the case for positive symptoms. Their research shows that some benefits of having CBT do last for two years. They also estimate that the cost of providing CBT was compensated for by patients spending less time in hospital. The research shows that CBT is an effective treatment for schizophrenia, and lasts for up to two years for some symptoms and functioning.

Summary of clinical psychology

In this chapter, we have focused on the field of clinical psychology. Clinical psychology assesses, diagnoses and treats people who are suffering from psychological disorders, as well as doing research into these disorders. See Box 9.5 for recent research in clinical psychology. One limitation in this field is that there is an element of judgement in diagnosing people with disorders; it is not always possible to do a laboratory test, as in medicine for physical illnesses. Nevertheless, clinical psychology has contributed enormously to people's well-being and quality of life by its practical applications, such as developing new treatments for mental disorders and preventions for addictions.

 Box 9.5 Research: other research in clinical psychology

Lange, Tierney, Reinhardt-Rutland and Vivekananda-Schmidt (2004): Looking at spiders
Do people who have a phobia of spiders spend more time looking at them? Lange *et al.* (2004) conducted a laboratory experiment at the University of Ulster in Northern Ireland to investigate this matter. Previous research had shown mixed findings; one study indicated that spider phobics pay less attention to a spider, whereas another study found that phobics directed their attention towards a spider more. In their study, Lange *et al.* (2004) used a real spider and a direct way of tracing where a person looks (attends). They propose that a phobic will pay more attention to a real spider than a picture, as a real spider can move toward

the phobic. It is also more ecologically valid. They used equipment that can record where a person looks in real time by tracking their eye movements. They recruited 32 participants who had completed the Spider Phobia Questionnaire (SPQ; Watts and Sharrock, 1984) which measures their vigilance and preoccupation, and how they cope with/avoid spiders. High and low scorers were used to form two groups: phobics and non-phobics (the control group).

During the experiment, the participants wore eye-tracking equipment (two miniature cameras on a headband) and were asked to watch a video on TV. They were incorrectly given the impression that the video content was an important part of the experiment. There were two shelves on the wall, two metres to the left and right of the TV. The left shelf was immediately next to the door, which was the only exit from the room (so it would be seen as something of safety). The right shelf was not next to a door. They used a tarantula spider in a sealed, transparent plastic box; participants were reassured that it could not get out. When the spider was placed on the left shelf, it was immediately next to the door, so safety and threat were placed together. When the spider was on the right shelf, it was not next to the door, so safety and threat were separated. They measured how long the person gazed at each of the TV, right shelf and left shelf/door as well as the number of eye movements made between these. They found that phobics viewed the TV less when the spider was present, increased viewing of the spider and exit, and showed the most change in viewing when the spider and exit were together. Also, the phobics made more shifts in gaze in presence of the spider, suggesting that they increased their scanning of the environment in general. This study therefore supports previous research that phobics do look more.

Milgrom, Negri, Gemmill, McNeil and Martin (2005): Treating postnatal depression
Postnatal depression (PND) affects at least one in ten new mothers and is a deep and long-term depression. Many women are offered antidepressants to treat their PND but are not willing to take these, for such reasons as the drugs' side effects or that they are breast-feeding. Milgrom and colleagues conducted research to look at alternative treatments for PND. They were interested in how effective psychological treatments (interventions) are compared to routine care. They compared routine care (the control condition) to three psychological interventions of group-based CBT, group counselling and individual counselling. They measured the effects of these interventions on anxiety and depression (anxiety frequently goes together with PND).

New mothers were recruited to complete a questionnaire which screens for PND. They were then clinically assessed by a psychologist to determine if they had a DSM-IV diagnosis of depression; 192 women had moderately severe PND. Their anxiety and depression levels were measured before they began treatment in order to get a baseline. The women were then randomly allocated to one of four treatments: group-based CBT, group-based counselling, individual counselling or routine care. Each of the psychological interventions was specifically developed to treat PND. The women had nine, weekly, 90-minute sessions.

The women's anxiety and depression were measured again at 12 weeks after treatment and they were followed-up after 12 months. Milgrom *et al.* (2005) did not find a difference in effectiveness between counselling or CBT, but did find that both counselling and CBT were more effective for treating PND than routine care. They conclude that psychological intervention is better than routine care for reducing depression and anxiety in PND.

PART 3
Reviewing psychology

Part 3 of this book consists of two chapters. In Chapter 10, we focus on how ethical issues are dealt with when doing psychology research, and look at a piece of research that is famous for the ethical issues it raised. The book concludes in Chapter 11 by reviewing what has been covered. It also looks at how research focus changes over time and provides information about studying psychology and careers in psychology.

10 The ethics of psychology research

As psychology is about examining human behaviour and mental processes, it is necessary to use human participants in research if we want to obtain findings which are valid. Using people comes with the responsibility to consider and protect their physical and mental well-being, and rights to privacy. Ethical guidelines have been put in place to ensure this. This chapter explains what the ethical guidelines are and how they are applied in order to protect participants. It also focuses on one research paper to highlight the issues of treating participants ethically.

What are ethics?

Ethics are a set of principles which relate to correct conduct and standards. They are related to a moral code which specifies right and wrong. In general, ethical codes set out rules for how specialists in a subject (e.g. medical doctors, lawyers, psychologists) should treat the general public. Ethical guidelines are there to protect the rights of a person, such as their privacy, safety and mental health.

Imagine the following scenario. You go into work one morning, as normal, and you are called to a meeting during which your employer tells you that you will be taking part in some research that two psychologists are doing. You are told that you must take part; the penalty for not doing so is to lose some of your monthly salary. One of the psychologists takes you to a room; you sit next to this psychologist who tells you to follow their instructions while the second psychologist observes you. You feel very uncomfortable with what they ask you to do, but when you ask to stop taking part, you are told that you cannot. Once the research is finished, you are told that you can go. You are not told anything about what you have just done. Over the next month, you feel anxious about what you did. How would you feel if this happened to you? Most probably, you would feel angry that you did not have a say in what you did, and that you were coerced into taking part. You may also be distressed that it had a lasting impact on you, leaving you with stress and anxiety.

Could this type of scenario really happen? Reassuringly, the answer is a definite 'no'. Psychology research is always conducted following strict guidelines to ensure that it is done ethically, to protect the participants. The events in the imaginary scenario violate just about all of the ethical guidelines to which psychologists must stick! For example, no one taking part in research is ever coerced into doing so; participation is always voluntary and the person is always informed about what they will be required to do. All research ends with a debriefing during which it is explained what they have done and why, and is an opportunity to ask any questions. Participants also have the right to stop the data gathered from them being used at any time after the research has been done.

The development of ethical guidelines

In the 1980s, there was growing concern and thought about ethics in psychology research. It was increasingly recognized that people taking part had rights and that these people were thinking and reasoning, not just passive entities to be manipulated. Up to and during the 1960s some studies were published which highlighted a lack of ethical treatment of participants, such as ignoring their rights (see Box 10.1). You may come across such studies when learning about psychology. It is important to recognize that these were conducted in a different social context and that psychology has moved on. Psychology courses now teach students about how to conduct research ethically.

What are the ethical guidelines?

Psychological Societies, such as the BPS, APA and EFPA, set out ethical principles for conducting psychological research. These ethical principles are guidelines or 'rules' about how to deal with ethical issues. Psychologists follow these ethical guidelines to protect their participants' safety, mental health and privacy. These also provide guidelines for advertising professional services and using **penile plethysmography**. All psychologists doing research must abide by these guidelines. They are also required to work within the Data Protection Act (1998) so that they act responsibly with personal information. Ethics guidelines are constantly reviewed to reflect changing social attitudes. Table 1.1 (see p. 9) briefly summarizes these guidelines. Box 10.2 goes into more detail, showing how psychologists deal with these guidelines in their research. Box 10.3 summarizes the guidelines for working with non-human animals – in this chapter we will only focus on working with humans.

Box 10.1 Research: examples of ethically controversial research studies

Walster (1965): Self-esteem and romantic liking
Walster examined whether a person's self-esteem at that moment affects how open they are to affection offered by another person. It was expected that a person with high self-esteem at the time, would be more open to affection than a person with low self-esteem. In the research, female participants were given false feedback on information from personality tests they had done. Half of the participants were given false information to raise their self-esteem and the other half to lower their self-esteem. A male confederate then asked them for a date. The women later rated the attractiveness of the young male confederate. Those with lower self-esteem expressed more liking for the confederate than those in high self-esteem group. The ethical issues this study raises are that it uses deception by using the male confederate and providing false feedback on their personality. Also, it is not pleasant for the participants to have their self-esteem raised/lowered. This would not be acceptable to do nowadays.

Haney, Banks and Zimbardo (1973): Prison simulation
Haney *et al.* (1973) conducted an experiment at Stanford University in which participants were placed in a simulated prison, as either prisoners or guards. The prisoner participants were arrested by real police at their homes by surprise. They were then taken to the 'prison', blindfolded, stripped and given prison uniform to wear. The prisoners were to be kept in prison for 24 hours a day, for 14 days. The participant guards were given instructions to maintain a reasonable degree of order and were not allowed to use physical violence. The researchers assessed the effects on behaviour by tape observation, self-report questionnaires and interviews. The experiment was terminated early after six days because half of the prisoners were showing signs of depression, fits of rage, acute anxiety and so on. The guards had enjoyed their power and behaved aggressively, abusing and dehumanizing the prisoners.

The study was ethically approved beforehand. Also, the participants gave their informed consent beforehand, signing a document stating that some of their rights would be suspended (e.g. privacy) and that they would all receive 15 dollars a day for up to two weeks. However, the study raises many ethical issues, particularly the distress and anxiety caused to the participant prisoners. Some details were withheld: the participants were not aware that they would be arrested in public or how realistic the imprisonment would be. Nevertheless, the researchers did stop the study early and participants had debriefing sessions and were assessed weeks, months and years afterwards.

Box 10.2 Details: ethical guidelines

The ethical guidelines set out by the BPS are summarized here (guidelines by the APA and EFPA are very similar). The summary describes what they are and how psychologists deal with these guidelines in their research.

Informed consent
Researchers must give participants detailed information about what they will experience in the research, so that they can agree/refuse to take part. The researchers must inform participants of the research objectives and, any aspects that might influence their willingness to take part. The more risks involved in the experiment, the more participants should be informed. There are different types of consent. Opt-in consent is when participants sign a statement saying that they are willing to take part. Opt-out consent is when participants are automatically included in the research, unless they sign a statement saying that they are not willing to take part. Opt-in consent is preferred. Sometimes researchers use presumptive consent. This is where, before the research happens, members of the population, from which participants are drawn, are asked how acceptable the research is. For children or adults with impairments, consent must come from either themselves (real consent) or parents/guardians. Researchers must remember that participants may see them as being in authority; they must not pressurize participants. They should not use payment to induce participants to risk harm.

Deception
This involves misleading participants. Active deception is where the experimenters deliberately mislead the participants about some feature of the experiment. Passive deception is where researchers mislead by withholding information. Researchers must avoid deception unless there is strong justification. While not all deception is unacceptable, it is if participants will object once they have been debriefed. If it is impossible to conduct the study without deception, participants must have sufficient information at the earliest stage. The researchers must consider the way that participants will feel about the deception.

Protection of participants from harm
Participants must be protected from both physical and psychological harm. Physical harm includes such factors as excessive anxiety. Psychological harm includes such factors as loss of self-esteem or embarrassment. There must be no more risk of harm than in ordinary life. Participants must be asked about factors that might create a risk (e.g. medical conditions) and be advised about how to avoid the risk. Researchers must inform participants about how they can contact the investigators should concerns arise after taking part. Researchers must protect the participants from stress if the study involves private/personal experiences

(e.g. assuring them that the answers are confidential). When working with children, researchers must be cautious about discussing results with parents/guardians as they may view information as being more significant than it really is.

Right to withdraw

Participants have the right to stop participating and/or to withdraw their data without any negative consequences (e.g. the researchers will still pay them). Participants (especially children) must know about their right to withdraw. When testing children, researchers must realize that a child avoiding the task is a sign that they do not wish to continue. All participants have the right to withdraw retrospectively (i.e. after debriefing) and for their own data to be destroyed.

Debriefing

This is providing participants with information about the nature and purpose of the research. The researchers should discuss the participant's experience of the study, to look out for any misunderstanding or negative consequences. Debriefing can compensate for using deception but it is not a justification for unethical research. A verbal debriefing may not be enough; researchers should also consider a more active debriefing method before the participants leave the research setting.

Confidentiality

It is a legal requirement (under the Data Protection Act) that all information obtained is confidential.

All information must be confidential unless otherwise agreed in advance. If information is published, it must not be identifiable. If the researchers cannot guarantee confidentiality/anonymity, they must warn participants before they give their consent.

Observational research

Studies involving observation must respect the participants' privacy and psychological well-being.

If people know that they are being observed, researchers must get their consent. If the people do not know, the research must only be done in situations where people would expect to be observed by strangers anyway.

Giving advice

The researchers may detect psychological or physical problems, or participants may seek advice. If the researchers detect any psychological/physical problems that the participant is not aware of, they have a responsibility to inform the participant if not doing so would endanger their future well-being. Researchers must be careful if a participant seeks advice. If they are not qualified to help, they should recommend an appropriate source of professional advice.

Colleagues
Researchers share the responsibility to treat participants ethically. If a researcher believes that another is not doing the research ethically, they should encourage them to do so.

 Box 10.3 Details: a summary of ethical issues for psychology research with non-human animals

The BPS ethical guidelines cover the use of animals for research, psychology teaching and therapy (e.g. treating phobias). The guidelines require psychologists to consider alternatives to using animals. However, if the benefits of using animals outweigh the costs, then researchers must minimize suffering and the number of animals used. Researchers must follow the guidelines:

- Researchers must follow the Animals (Scientific Procedures) Act 1986 and laws for animal welfare.
- Researchers must choose a species that is well suited for the research and is the least likely to suffer.
- Researchers are legally required to use the smallest number of animals necessary.
- If any procedure has an adverse effect on the animal, this must be recognized, assessed and immediate action taken. The guidelines cover the following procedures:

1   Reward, deprivation and aversive stimulation – researchers must not deprive animals of food or other needs.
2   Isolation and crowding – social animals find isolation stressful whereas crowding has negative effects (e.g. aggression).
3   Aggression and predation – researchers must ensure that there is no aggression between animals.
4   Fieldwork – researchers must minimize interference with free-living animals and their ecosystems.
5   Anaesthesia, analgesia and euthanasia – researchers must use proper pre- and post-operative care to minimize stress.

- Animals must come from Home Office Designated Breeding and Supply Establishments.
- Researchers are responsible for all of the animal's needs and welfare (e.g. cage cleaning, good food).
- Reuse of animals is very controlled. Death must be humane and under a vet's guidance.

Applying ethics involves judgement, so before beginning any research project, the researchers involved must first present their research proposal to an ethics committee, where it is scrutinized. The proposal must get approval from an ethics committee before research can begin. All psychology institutions, where research is being carried out, have an ethics committee. Ideally, the committee also includes non-psychologists so that there is not a bias. The committee considers and evaluates whether, for instance, the proposed research is a topic worth investigating, that it will not cause harm, whether there will be any problems with participants giving informed consent and so on. If working with children or vulnerable adults, the researchers need to be cleared by a criminal record check. An individual who violates these guidelines is not committing a crime, but their psychological society can bar them from membership. We will now turn to a renowned research paper which illustrates some of the issues surrounding ethics in research.

Research paper

Stanley Milgram (1933–1984) is a well-known name in psychology, particularly for one research study done at Yale University (USA) in 1963. The research study is famous because of its procedure and how it was responded to. Stanley Milgram conducted research into one aspect of social influence: obedience. He was specifically interested in the extent to which people would follow orders. We will look at his research paper before discussing the ethical issues it raises.

The paper

Milgram, S. (1963) Behavioural study of obedience, *Journal of Abnormal and Social Psychology*, 67(4): 371–8.

Milgram was interested in obedience, which is a fundamental part of living in a society. He was particularly inspired by the events of the Second World War. In his paper, he states:

> Obedience, as a determinant of behaviour, is of particular relevance to our time. It has been reliably established that from 1933–45, millions of innocent people were systematically slaughtered on command. Gas chambers were built, death camps were guarded, daily quotas of corpses were produced with the same efficiency as the manufacture of appliances. These inhumane policies may have originated in the mind of a single person, but they could only be carried out on a massive scale if a very large number of people obeyed orders.
>
> (Milgram, 1963: 371)

Milgram suggests that obedience may be so deeply ingrained that it can override our moral codes. He states that 'the individual who is commanded by a legitimate authority ordinarily obeys. Obedience comes easily and often. It is a ubiquitous and indispensable feature of social life' (Milgram, 1963: 372).

He set out to investigate how much people would obey an authority figure when asked to inflict pain on another person. He describes his participants (subjects) as follows:

> The subjects were 40 males between the ages of 20 and 50, drawn from New Haven and the surrounding communities. Subjects were obtained by a newspaper advertisement and direct mail solicitation. Those who responded to the appeal believed that they were to participate in a study of memory and learning at Yale University. A wide range of occupations was represented in the sample. Typical subjects were postal clerks, high school teachers, salesmen, engineers and labourers. Subjects ranged in educational level from one who had not finished elementary school, to those who had doctorate and professional degrees. They were paid $4.50 for their participation in the experiment. However, subjects were told that payment was simply for coming to the laboratory, and that the money was theirs no matter what happened after they arrived.
>
> (Milgram, 1963: 372)

These participants were led to believe that the research was about the effect of punishment on learning. In fact, the laboratory experiment was investigating obedience and involved three people: the naïve participant (subject), who acts as the teacher; a confederate, who pretends to be the experimenter; and another confederate, who pretends to be another participant and acts as the learner (victim). The experimenter confederate was played by a 31-year-old high-school teacher, dressed in a laboratory coat. His manner was impassive and stern throughout the experiment. The confederate learner was played by a 47-year-old male accountant, who appeared mild-mannered and likeable.

The experiment required the naïve participant to act as a teacher, punishing the learner's mistakes by giving them electric shocks. The naïve participants were given a 'cover story' about what was happening; they were told that:

> We want to find out just what effect different people have on each other as teachers and learners, and also what effect punishment will have on learning in this situation. Therefore, I'm going to ask one of you to be the teacher here tonight and the other one to be the learner. Does either of you have a preference?
>
> (Milgram, 1963: 373)

The naïve participant and confederate participant then drew slips of paper, from a hat, to determine who would be the teacher and learner. However, this was rigged so that the naïve participant was always the teacher and the confederate participant was always the learner. Both were then taken to an adjacent room and the learner was strapped into a chair with electrodes attached to his wrists. They participants were told that the electrodes were attached to an electric shock generator in the next room. They were also told 'Although the shocks can be extremely painful, they cause no permanent tissue damage' (Milgram, 1963: 373). Milgram describes the electric shock generator as:

> The instrument panel consists of 30 lever switches set in a horizontal line. Each switch is clearly labelled with a voltage designation that ranges from 15 to 450 volts. There is a 15-volt increment from one switch to the next going from left to right. In addition, the following verbal designations are clearly indicated for groups of four switches going from left to right: Slight Shock, Moderate Shock, Strong Shock, Very Strong Shock, Intense Shock, Extreme Intensity Shock, Danger: Severe Shock. (Two switches after this last designation are simply marked XXX).
>
> (Milgram, 1963: 373)

The teacher was taken to the room with the shock generator and instructed to deliver an electric shock to the learner for each incorrect answer to a word association test. The teacher was to move one level higher each time the learner gave the wrong answer. The learner communicated his answers through an answering device; these were actually standardized responses and included frequent incorrect responses. When the 300 volt shock was given, the learner pounded on the wall and then nothing more was heard from him. If the participant teacher showed any reluctance to continue, the experimenter instructed the teacher to continue with standardized prompts (prods) said in a firm but polite voice. These included:

> Prod 1: Please continue *or* Please go on. Prod 2: The experiment requires that you continue. Prod 3: It is absolutely essential that you continue. Prod 4: You have no other choice, you *must* go on.
>
> (Milgram, 1963: 374)

The experiment was always terminated after prod 4. Once the experiment was terminated, the participant was interviewed and debriefed. Milgram describes this:

> Following the experiment, subjects were interviewed; open-ended

questions, projective measures and attitude scales were employed. After the interview, procedures were undertaken to assure that the subject would leave the laboratory in a state of well-being. A friendly reconciliation was arranged between the subject and the victim, and an effort was made to reduce any tensions that arose as a result of the experiment.

(Milgram, 1963: 374)

The main dependent variable was the maximum shock the participant administered before refusing to go on. Other measures included observations made through one-way mirrors and notes on unusual behaviours. Most experimental sessions were recorded on tape. In the results section of his paper, Milgram first describes how he asked others to predict the likely outcomes of the experiment before it was done:

Fourteen Yale seniors, all psychology majors, were provided with a detailed description of the experimental situation. They were asked to reflect carefully on it, and to predict the behaviour of 100 hypothetical subjects. More specifically, they were instructed to plot the distribution of obedience of '100 Americans of diverse occupations, and ranging in age from 20 to 50 years,' who were placed in the experiment situation.

(Milgram, 1963: 375)

All respondents predicted that only a minority of people (three per cent at most) would go to the end of the shock series to reach 450 volts. Milgram's colleagues predicted that few, if any, would go to beyond the level of Very Strong Shock. The actual results of the experiment showed that obedience was greater than predicted. Of the 40 participants, 26 (65 per cent) obeyed the experimenter's orders to the end, continuing to the maximum shock level (450 volts). All participants gave shocks up to the 300 volt level (Intense Shock). Of the 40 subjects, five refused to go beyond 300 volts, four more went one level further and then refused to go on. A total of 14 participants defied the experimenter. It was found that the naïve participants did believe the experimental setup. In a post-experimental interview, participants were asked 'How painful to the learner were the last few shocks that you administered to him?' The mean response was 13.42 out of a 14 point scale (14 being 'extremely painful'). It was also seen that the experiment caused much tension in the participants. During the experiment, signs of the participants' tension included nervous laughing fits, sweating, trembling, stuttering, groaning and digging fingers into their own flesh.

Milgram states that there are two surprising aspects of his findings. First, the level of obedience is much stronger than expected, and was not predicted in the pre-experiment questioning. Second, the extraordinary tension the procedure generated in the participant had not been anticipated. He explains the high level of obedience as possibly being due a number of factors, such as: the experiment is being done at Yale University which the participants see as having authority; the experiment is supposedly about learning which is a worthy purpose; and the participant has entered the experiment voluntarily and feels obliged to the experimenter.

The response to Milgram's (1963) research

Milgram's study created much controversy as it showed that 'ordinary' people were so obedient to authority that they would give electric shocks to a stranger and that a fairly large proportion of people would even give up to 450 volts. His research was severely criticized for breaking ethical guidelines in four areas. We will look at each of these in turn.

Protection from harm
The ethical guidelines state that participants must be protected from harm and should not be distressed in any way by the procedure. Baumrind (1964) criticized Milgram's (1963) research for causing severe distress to the participants.

Deception
Ethical guidelines state that researchers should avoid deception unless there is extremely strong scientific justification for deceiving participants. Milgram is criticized for not telling his participants the true purpose of their role in the study. They also believed that the shocks were real.

Lack of informed consent
The guidelines state that participants must give their informed consent to take part themselves and that they know what is going to happen during the experiment. A criticism of Milgram's study is that it was not possible to obtain the participants' informed consent because they did not have full knowledge about what was going to happen. This is because the study involved deception.

The right to withdraw
Ethical guidelines state that participants have the right to withdraw, which is the freedom to leave or stop the experiment at any time. It is argued that Milgram did not tell the participants that they had the right to stop. He supports this by the fact that the experimenter ordered participants to continue.

Milgram's response

It would therefore appear that Milgram contravened some of the major ethical guidelines. In fact, Milgram did consider these issues and defended his research on these issues as follows.

Protection from harm

Milgram argued that he had not anticipated there being any distress before beginning the experiments. He did conduct an extensive follow-up of the participants one year after the study. He found that they did not appear to have suffered any harm or distress. Eighty-four per cent said that they were glad to have participated, 15 per cent were neutral whereas only 1.3 per cent were sorry that they had participated. Furthermore, when psychiatrists interviewed 40 participants one year after the study, they found that the study had caused no harm.

Deception

Milgram countered this criticism by stating that the deception was necessary, otherwise the task would not seem real to the participants and this would affect the end results. Milgram did debrief his participants and reassure them by introducing them to the confederate learner at the end. He also assured them that their behaviour was normal.

Lack of informed consent

Milgram did get 'presumptive consent' in which people were asked beforehand if they thought that a study would be acceptable to do. Milgram could not have anticipated the surprising results of the experiment.

The right to withdraw

Milgram did inform participants that they could leave and that they would get their money regardless. Milgram argued that participants were free to leave as they were not physically restrained.

How else can we evaluate Milgram's (1963) study?

Milgram did follow ethical procedures and provided much care in the follow-up study to assess the participants' responses to being involved in the experiment. Indeed, Milgram was ahead of his time in using ethical scrutiny; he pioneered ethical committees, which are now taken for granted (Blass, 2004). It should be remembered that the findings of his study were not predicted, so he did find something of value. Milgram's findings did contribute to current thinking about obedience at the time. Also, they have had a great impact on experimental research and theory since. The majority of obedience studies conducted since Milgram's (1963) have involved some form of breaking the ethical guidelines (e.g. using deception). Baumrind (1964) suggests that the general population reacted strongly to Milgram's findings as they did not want to accept the implications that 'ordinary' people could be so obedient as to cause harm to others. So they responded by shifting attention from the results to attacking the ethics used instead. Likewise, Aronson (1988) claims that there would be no ethical objections to the study if the findings were more acceptable.

Summary of the ethics of psychology research

Psychology cannot advance its understanding of human behaviour without having people take part in research. Ethical guidelines have been put in place to protect the rights of participants. These ethical guidelines are constantly reviewed to reflect changing social attitudes (for example, the BPS revised their ethical guidelines in 2006). It should be kept in mind that applying ethical guidelines to research is not a straightforward case of sticking to rigid rules, but requires judgement. For instance, deception does not allow participants to be fully informed, but being fully informed can decrease the effectiveness of a study. Furthermore, some psychologists propose that using deception in research can make the public suspicious about psychology research. However, there is evidence that most people do not object to the use of deception (Kimmel, 1998) and see taking part in research as an educational experience (Christensen, 1988).

11 Conclusion

This chapter concludes the book by first reviewing what we have learnt in the previous chapters. We will then look at psychology in a broader light, by briefly exploring one issue to show how the research focus changes over time. Finally, we will look at how you can go about studying psychology and how to become a psychologist.

Review of the book

The aim of this book was to introduce you to psychology by giving you a flavour of what psychology is. In Part 1, we described what psychology is and looked at how psychology research is done and how the findings are written as research papers. In Part 2, we reviewed a selection of topics encompassed by psychology, using one piece of research in detail from each of the core areas of psychology. The purpose of looking at one paper was to give you a 'taster' of that area and how the research is done. In Part 3, we looked at how ethical issues are dealt with in psychology research. We will now review the major points covered in each chapter.

Part 1

Chapter 1

- Psychology is the systematic study of minds and behaviour.
- Psychology came to be a distinct subject in the mid-nineteenth century.
- Our understanding of behaviour and minds, is based on evidence from research.
- Psychology is a broad subject involving a variety of approaches. These approaches include cognitive, social, developmental, biological,

learning, evolutionary, psychodynamic and humanistic approaches (see Table 1.2, p. 13).

- Psychology not only investigates our behaviour, it also helps people in such ways as developing methods for overcoming phobias, increasing road safety and reducing prejudice.

Chapter 2

- Psychologists find out facts about human behaviour by collecting information.
- The different ways of collecting information are known as research methods (e.g. questionnaires, observations and laboratory experiments).
- Understanding research involves knowing the key terms (e.g. hypotheses, variables).
- Statistical tests are used to see whether the finding is significant (how probable it is that the finding occurred by chance).

Chapter 3

- Research findings are reported in journals as a research paper (research findings are also presented at conferences). These papers undergo peer review to ensure their quality.
- Research papers are important in order for knowledge to advance; journal publication allows for research to be replicated and the findings to be assessed and discussed.
- Research papers are written using the same format.

Part 2

The chapters in Part 2 each dipped into one area of psychology. Each chapter examined what that area encompasses and looked at one piece of research in depth, using the original research paper.

Chapter 4

- Cognitive psychology explains our behaviour by viewing it in terms of what is going on in our minds (our mental processes). It examines how we take in and mentally process information.
- The research paper by Loftus and Palmer (1974) investigated memory. It showed that our memory for an event can be influenced by information we receive after the event.

Chapter 5

- Social psychology views our behaviour in its social context. It examines how people influence other people's behaviour, thoughts and emotions.
- The research paper by Fischer *et al.* (2006) investigated pro-social behaviour, specifically people's helping behaviour. Their research showed that the context people are in determines whether they will help others.

Chapter 6

- Developmental psychology examines how we develop over our lifespan, from conception to old age.
- The research paper by Bokhorst *et al.* (2003) examined the type of attachment that develops between an infant and its mother. It showed that the environment plays an important role in differences in attachment types, whereas genetics play only a small role.

Chapter 7

- Biological psychology views our behaviour in terms of our underlying biological processes.
- The research paper by McDaniel (2005) looked at whether the size of our brains relates to how intelligent we are. His meta-analysis confirmed that the bigger the brain, the higher the intelligence.

Chapter 8

- The area of individual differences examines the psychological similarities and differences between people.
- The research by Costa and McCrae (1988) examined whether our personality changes or stays the same throughout adulthood. Their evidence suggests that personality is stable after age 30.

Chapter 9

- Clinical psychology researches into, and is concerned with, the assessment, diagnosis and treatment of mental disorders.
- The research paper by Startup *et al.* (2005) examined the benefits of cognitive-behavioural therapy for schizophrenia over two years. They found that CBT is an effective treatment for schizophrenia and the benefits persist for some symptoms and functioning for two years.

Part 3

Chapter 10

- Ethical guidelines are used in order to protect the well-being and rights of people taking part in research.
- Milgram's (1963) research study into obedience highlights some of the issues of treating participants ethically.

Summary

To give you a taste of psychology, the chapters have covered a widespread range of topics. You have learnt about:

- how threatening things (such as a snarling dog) are generally not detected any more quickly than non-threatening ones (e.g. a plant);
- how your memory can be inaccurate, being affected by information after an event;
- how people may or may not help others depending on the presence of bystanders and the situation they are in;
- how the type of bond you have with your parent/child appears to be largely determined by your environment rather than your genes;
- how the size of your brain relates to how intelligent you are, depending on your age and gender;
- how your personality appears to stay the same throughout your adult life;
- how one type of 'talking therapy' (CBT) is an effective way of helping people with schizophrenia for at least two years;
- how ordinary people will obey orders from an authority figure to a surprising degree.

The 'other research' in boxes has covered additional topics, such as if group brainstorming works, if being a grandparent makes you feel younger and if we actually 'feel' other people's pain.

The chapters have also covered an assortment of ways in which research is done. The research methods include:

- laboratory experiments to investigate how well we visually spot something threatening, how leading questions affect how well we remember an event and the extent to which people will obey orders;
- a natural experiment where the participants are people who suffer from schizophrenia;
- observations to note whether participants try to help someone, to

determine which type of attachment a child has with its mother, and to record people's behaviour when asked to give electric shocks to another person;

- questionnaires to assess how people felt about helping someone in an emergency and to assess a child's temperament;
- structured interviews to assess the symptoms and functioning of people suffering from schizophrenia;
- a twin study to assess how much environment or genes influence the type of attachment a child has with its mother;
- psychometric tests to assess intelligence and personality;
- a meta-analysis to integrate the findings from many previous research studies;
- correlations of brain size with intelligence;
- longitudinal and cross-sectional methods to assess how stable personality is.

It is important to remember that each piece of research mentioned in this book is only one from a huge array done on that particular topic. Other research may agree with and support these findings, but can equally contradict them. Questioning the findings and doing further research is normal in trying to establish the 'facts'. Without this, knowledge would not advance. Some of the topics covered in this book are involved in ongoing debates. For example, there is a long-standing debate into how stable personality is in adulthood. Costa and McCrae's longitudinal research suggests that personality is stable. However, Ardelt (2000) states that personality is found to be less stable when the length of time between the two personality assessments is of twenty years or more and if the person is under 30 years old or over 50 years old at the first assessment. It is also important to note that any one research method can be used in a number of areas. For example, a longitudinal method is used in both the research in individual differences (Chapter 8) and in clinical psychology (Chapter 9). Also, a mixture of methods can be used in any one research study, for example an observation and questionnaires are used in the research into attachment (Chapter 6).

A brief exploration of consciousness

Which particular topics are examined in psychology changes over time; some topics go in and out of fashion, depending on such factors as society's views at that time and the research methods available. We will now briefly explore one topic, consciousness, to illustrate how the research focus alters with time and how the methods available can advance research in any one topic.

What is consciousness?

Our consciousness is a fundamental part of being human. We can say that a rock is not conscious, an insect may be, yet we definitely are. What consciousness is, and where it is located, has puzzled us for a long time. Before we look at how this topic has been considered and studied over time, we need to define what it is. In psychology and philosophy, consciousness is defined as our awareness. For example, we have a conscious experience and awareness of seeing the colour blue. We can think of consciousness as our awareness of something we are attending to, whereas we are unconscious of things outside of our focused attention. Psychology and philosophy do *not* think about consciousness in terms of Freud's theory (where our unconscious mind holds our inner desires and repressed experiences).

We can turn to neuropsychology for evidence that we process some information consciously but other information unconsciously. Neuropsychology is concerned with the role that particular areas of the brain play in various behaviours. It examines this by looking at how damage to specific areas of the brain affects behaviour, resulting in deficits (e.g. loss of the ability to recognize faces). Neuropsychology largely uses case studies of brain-damaged individuals, some of which are now 'classic' cases. One such case is of DB (the person is always referred to by their initials). DB had a non-malignant tumour surgically removed from the right side of his brain (in an area that processes vision) when he was 26 years old.

After the operation, DB was left with a region of blindness in the left field of vision, called a blindfield. When he was tested by Weiskrantz and colleagues (e.g. Weiskrantz, 1986) it was found that DB was not aware of anything in his blindfield. However, he could make eye movements to a light flashed in his blindfield, even though he was not aware of seeing it. DB could also reach towards a stimulus and distinguish X from O in his blindfield. He was astonished at his own performance. The ability that DB shows is known as 'blindsight'.

Blindsight occurs when there is damage specifically to an area at the back of the brain called the primary visual cortex (or V1) which processes visual information. The person is blind due to damage to their brain, not because there is something wrong with their eyes. When this person is shown a stimulus in their blindfield, they say that they have seen nothing, as you would expect. Yet when asked to react to stimuli by, for example, saying which of two objects they have been shown, they are able to perform better than chance. They perform accurately despite not being aware of seeing anything. This disorder shows that although the person with blindsight has no conscious experience of seeing anything, they can still respond to it. This is possible because other parts of the brain, that also deal with visual processing, can unconsciously process the stimuli, allowing the person to detect it.

A distinction between conscious awareness and unconscious processing is also shown in the research by Whalen *et al.* (1998) in Chapter 7. Their research showed that a part of the brain, the amygdala, reacts to emotional faces even when the person is not aware of having seen an emotional face.

How has consciousness been investigated over time?

When psychology first became a scientific discipline in the nineteenth century, the main interest was in consciousness and subjective experience. Wilhelm Wundt (1832–1920), the German physiologist, regarded the conscious mind as the primary object to examine. He believed that we could gain information about how people's minds were working by using **introspection**. Wundt used introspection in the first psychology laboratory which he set up in Leipzig in 1879. However, by the early twentieth century, psychologists had concluded that consciousness could not be studied scientifically. The behaviourist approach in psychology, which was dominant from 1913 to the 1950s, was against using introspection to investigate subjective experience. They argued that psychology should be based on the experimental study of behaviour, not on a person's judgements about their own feelings. Instead, behaviourists focused only on observable behaviours (what is going on in our mind is not directly observable). Behaviourism prevented consciousness being considered in psychology for almost half a century. The study of consciousness was left to philosophy.

The study of consciousness had returned to psychology by 1968, when Roger Sperry (1913–1994) showed that consciousness can be studied in the laboratory under controlled conditions. He used an experimental method to examine conscious awareness in the two halves (hemispheres) of the brain. He examined conscious awareness in patients who had had the two hemispheres surgically separated to alleviate severe epilepsy (called split-brain patients). Sperry's research showed that each hemisphere can have its own independent conscious experience. A massive increase in research and theorizing on consciousness happened in the 1990s. One of the big issues in consciousness now is to determine which brain areas are active during conscious awareness. The brain states that occur when a person experiences certain conscious states are known as 'neural correlates of consciousness' (NCCs). Developments in neuroscience and improved brain scanning mean that we can now look at the brain in detail when it is active and so search for NCCs. Our knowledge has advanced to the point that we know that there is not one area of consciousness in the brain, but many possible NCCs. One possible NCC, for example, is the primary visual cortex (V1) which is associated with the conscious experience of seeing something.

Summary

How consciousness has been investigated in psychology over time shows how research interests go in and out of favour, and how advances in knowledge are tied in with advances in research methods and technology.

Studying and careers in psychology

Studying psychology

Psychology can be studied in many settings, including schools, colleges and universities, as well as in adult education centres and by distance learning. Psychology qualifications are offered at many levels. These include GCSE, AS level, A2 level, A level, Scottish Highers, SCOTVEC National Certificate modules and so on. Psychology can also be studied at degree level. At the time of writing, institutions offering psychology degrees do not ask for students to have any prior qualification in psychology. In fact, in the UK, a high number of students do not have A level psychology, and 30 per cent of new students are mature students (QAA 2000). If you are interested in studying for a psychology degree in the UK, you are strongly advised to ensure that the degree is an accredited course. This enables you to qualify for the 'Graduate Basis for Registration' (GBR) which is necessary to go on to further postgraduate training; it is needed before you can go on to be a **chartered psychologist**. If you plan to change careers to one in psychology or you are have a degree in a subject other than psychology, you will need to do a conversion course to qualify for the GBR. The BPS accredits courses in the UK and The Psychological Society of Ireland accredits courses in the Republic of Ireland.

Careers: How to become a psychologist

There are many types of psychologist. Training generally involves gaining a degree and then doing further training to specialize in one area. The main types of psychologist are as follows.

Psychology researchers and lecturers

Psychologists who work as university lecturers do both teaching and research. They work in universities, colleges and schools or in research units. To become a university lecturer, it is necessary to have an accredited degree with GBR and a **PhD** or to have held a research post. Lecturers also study for a Postgraduate Certificate in Higher Education. To teach psychology in a school, it is necessary to have a Postgraduate Certificate in Education. Some lecturers are qualified in one of the areas below and also do academic teaching and research.

Clinical psychologist

Clinical psychologists aim to reduce the psychological distress from mental disorders and to promote well-being. They work in health and social care settings, such as hospitals and community mental health services. To become a clinical psychologist it is necessary to have an accredited degree with GBR and to then do postgraduate training in clinical psychology over three years (full time).

Counselling psychologist

Counselling psychologists have trained in the assessment of mental health needs and therapy, which includes developing an understanding of their own personal history. Counselling psychologists work in industry, commerce, the prison service, education and so on. A counselling psychologist needs an accredited degree with GBR. They then do three years full-time postgraduate training in two/more types of therapy.

Educational psychologist

Educational psychologists work with individuals, from infants up to 19 year olds. They apply psychology to child development and learning. They mainly work in local education authorities, social services or privately. An accredited degree with GBR is needed to be an educational psychologist, along with teaching experience plus further training or the BPS approved postgraduate study, which is partly based on work placements.

Forensic psychologist

Forensic psychologists are involved in the psychological aspects of legal processes. For example, they deal with changing offender behaviour and crime analysis. They are largely employed by the prison service, but also work in social services and privately. A forensic psychologist needs an accredited degree with GBR, plus the BPS Diploma in Forensic Psychology which includes study and supervised practice.

Health psychologist

Health psychologists promote changes in people's behaviour and thinking about health and illness (e.g. developing interventions to prevent smoking). They work in hospitals, research units and so on. They need an accredited degree with GBR plus a master's degree (MSc) or the BPS qualification in Health Psychology.

Neuropsychologist

Neuropsychologists are involved in research into, and the assessment and rehabilitation of, people with brain damage/neurological problems. They work in such places as rehabilitation centres, hospitals and community services. To become a neuropsychologist, a person needs to have an accredited degree with GBR. They then undergo clinical psychology training plus supervised practice to qualify for the BPS Division of Neuropsychology Practitioner.

Occupational psychologist

Occupational psychologists apply psychology to work, being concerned with such issues as how working conditions affect people's behaviour. They work for large organizations in both the private and public sectors, and can work in consultancies. An occupational psychologist needs an accredited degree with GBR. They then need a BPS Master's degree in Occupational Psychology or a postgraduate certificate in occupational psychology. They also do supervised practice over two/three years.

Sport and exercise psychologist

Sport and exercise psychologists are concerned with the behaviour and mental processes of people involved in sport and exercise. They research into and help, for example, athletes mentally prepare for competition. Exercise psychologists are concerned with applying psychology to increase participation in exercise in the general population. Both work in a wide range of settings, such as professional sport teams, but they mostly do consultancy work.

It is important to know that, at present in the UK, anyone can call themselves a psychologist, regardless of whether they are qualified or not. However, to be a chartered psychologist, a person needs to have qualifications and training recognized by the BPS. This ensures that the person is fit to practise. It takes at least six years to be a chartered psychologist (three as an undergraduate and three in postgraduate education or training). The BPS holds a register of chartered psychologists.

Going on to other careers with a psychology degree

Although about 15 to 20 per cent of psychology graduates do go on to become professional psychologists, the remainder go into non-psychology fields. A psychology degree is useful for working in other areas, such as health, education, industry and commerce. In fact, the skills gained from a psychology degree are desirable in many other careers. For example, psychology graduates have learnt research skills, such as being able to plan and carry out a study efficiently. They are able to reason about data and present findings effectively.

They have communication skills, such as conveying ideas in writing, as well as doing spoken presentations to groups. They have effective team working skills, interpersonal skills (i.e. they know about the factors that affect behaviour and social interaction) and lifelong learning skills.

Summary of the book

Psychology is a fascinating subject that is relevant to us all. As you will have seen, it is an extremely wide-ranging subject which uses an extensive array of research methods. I hope that by reading this book you have gained more knowledge about the factors underlying our behaviour. If the research described in this book has raised as many issues as it answered, then I will be pleased, as I hope that this inspires you to continue learning about psychology and human behaviour!

Glossary

Affective Relating to emotion, moods and feelings.

Aim The aim of a piece of research is what is intended to be investigated.

American Psychological Association (APA) The organization that represents psychology in the United States. The APA aims to advance psychology as both a profession and a science.

Amygdala An almond-shaped structure located near the front of the brain which is involved in emotion and memory, particularly in attaching emotional significance to information.

Analysis of variance A statistical test which compares the means of different conditions, looking for differences between them (abbreviated to ANOVA).

Anecdote A short account about an incident or person, which can be hearsay or considered to be unreliable.

Anomaly Something that deviates from what is standard, normal or expected.

Apparatus Equipment needed for an investigation (e.g. a computer).

Artificial intelligence The development of computers to do tasks that are considered to require intelligence.

Attrition The process of being gradually worn down.

Average A usual or ordinary amount (the different calculations of the average are the mean, median and mode).

Between-participants (unrelated or independent-groups) design When participants are allocated to different conditions (cf within-participants design).

Brain-imaging techniques Techniques used to produce pictures of the brain, such as magnetic resonance imaging.

Brain-scanning When scanning equipment is used to produce images of the brain (e.g. magnetic resonance imaging).

Brainstorming Producing an idea or solution by thinking about or discussing it intensively (e.g. by having a group discussion).

British Psychological Society (BPS) The organization which represents psychology in the United Kingdom and is responsible for developing, promoting and applying psychology for the public's benefit.

Bystander A person who is present at an event or incident but does not take part.

Case study A detailed study of a particular person or group.

cf Abbreviation meaning 'compare with'.

Chartered psychologist A person who has a recognized degree and who has undergone approved postgraduate training and supervision in psychology. The person is deemed 'fit to practise' and follows a strict code of conduct. The British Psychological Society has been authorized by the Crown to run the Register of Chartered Psychologists to protect the public.

Chi-square A statistical test which measures the association between two variables (represented by the symbol χ^2).

Citation Reference to an author or a publication (e.g. a research paper or book).

Closed questions Questions which have a predetermined answer (e.g. yes/no).

Conditions Levels of the independent variable.

Confound/confounded A confound is a variable that is not part of the research but still has an effect on the findings. The study is said to be confounded if a variable that is not manipulated as part of the research has an effect on the findings.

Control In research, control is when factors are held constant or when an extraneous factor that might affect the results of an investigation is taken into account.

Control condition The condition which does not contain the factor being studied (cf experimental condition).

Cortex The deeply-folded outer layer of the brain (also called the cerebral cortex).

Counterbalancing Manipulating the order in which conditions are experienced, so that each condition precedes and follows every other condition an equal number of times.

Data Facts and statistics used for reference or analysis. Data is the plural of datum (Latin).

Demographic An attribute that characterizes a population (e.g. relating to wealth, deaths and so on).

Dependent variable The variable whose variation depends on that of another; the variable not manipulated by the researcher (cf independent variable).

Directional hypothesis Also called a one-tailed or uni-directional hypothesis. It predicts a difference between conditions and the direction of this difference (cf non-directional hypothesis).

Double-blind An investigation where information that may bias the results is concealed from both researcher and participant.

Ecological validity The extent to which the findings of an investigation generalize to real life settings.

Electro-convulsive therapy (ECT) When an electric shock is used to treat severe depression.

Electroencephalograph Equipment that measures electrical activity in the brain. An electroencephalogram (EEG) is the recording of the electrical activity.

Empathic Empathy is the ability to understand and share the feelings of another.

Et al. This is an abbreviation for the Latin term *et alia* which means 'and the others'. It is used in citations in the main text after the first author's surname when there are more than two authors for a work (in the Harvard referencing system).

Ethical Relates to ethics, which are a set of moral principles of right/wrong which apply to conduct. Ethical issues are dilemmas, such as whether it is acceptable to deceive a participant. Ethical guidelines are 'rules' set out by organizations about professional conduct and how to deal with such ethical issues.

European Federation of Psychologists' Associations (EFPA) The EFPA is the leading federation of European psychology associations which coordinates psychology training, practice and research. It has 32 member associations, representing about 180,000 psychologists.

Evidence Information indicating whether a proposition is true or valid.

Experimental condition The condition in which the suspected causal variable is present; the condition which contains the factor being studied (cf control condition).

Experimental hypothesis The hypothesis that predicts a difference on the dependent variable between conditions (see hypothesis; cf null hypothesis).

Extraneous variables Variables/influences which are unwanted causes or effects on the dependent variable.

Extraversion Being predominantly outgoing and socially confident.

Extraverts The personality type where the person is sociable and outgoing (cf introverts).

False memories A memory of an event that did not happen or a distorted memory of an event.

Functional magnetic resonance imaging (fMRI) A brain-imaging technique that detects magnetic changes in the flow of blood to brain cells.

Generalize Extending research findings to situations other than those directly assessed in the research (i.e. extrapolating from the sample tested to the whole population).

Genes A gene is a biological unit of heredity which transfers from parent to offspring. An organism's genetic makeup is encoded in their genes.

Genetics The study of inheritance of physical and psychological characteristics.

Genotype A person's genetic instructions given at conception (cf phenotype).

Gustatory To do with the sense of taste.

Heredity The passing on of physical or psychological characteristics genetically from one generation to another.

Hypothesis/hypotheses An idea or proposed explanation made on the basis of limited evidence as a starting point for further investigation.

Hysteria Exaggerated or uncontrolled emotion, or excitement. In psychiatry, an old-fashioned term for a psychological disorder where psychological stress is converted into physical symptoms.

Independent variable The variable whose variation does not depend on that of another; the variable manipulated by the researcher (cf dependent variable).

Intelligence quotient (IQ) The score on a measure of intelligence which represents a person's mental age divided by their chronological age (and then multiplied by 100 to remove any fractions). The average IQ is 100.

Intercoder reliability See inter-observer reliability.

Internal validity See validity.

Inter-observer reliability The extent of agreement between the scoring of more than one observer/scorer.

Intrinsic Belonging naturally to something; being essential.

Introspection Looking in at our own mental experience in order to break it down into parts.

Introverts The personality type where the person is shy, withdrawn and likes to be alone (cf extraverts).

In vivo In the living organism.

Labelling Attaching a label to a person which then defines them, possibly with adverse effects (e.g. labelling a person as unintelligent may lead to them being given fewer educational opportunities).

Lobotomies Surgically severing bands of nerves in the brain to treat certain mental disorders. These are rarely done nowadays.

Magnetic resonance imaging (MRI) A brain-imaging technique that scans the brain using magnetic fields and radio waves.

Magnetoencephalogram (MEG) A method of scanning the brain which measures very faint magnetic fields in the brain using supercooled, highly sensitive detectors positioned over the person's head.

Mania In psychology, a person with mania has copious and rapidly changing ideas, exaggerated sexuality, joy or irritability, and a decrease in sleep.

Manic Exhibiting mania.

Materials Things used in an investigation (e.g. pens, paper) (cf apparatus).

Mean The average of a set of quantities (calculated by adding amounts together and dividing the total by the number of amounts).

Motor Relating to movement.

Multiple personalities Multiple personality disorder is where a person has two or more distinct personalities that control behaviour. It is now called dissociative identity disorder (DID).

Neurology The branch of medicine and biology concerned with the nervous system.

Neurophysiological Relating to the physiology of the nervous system.

Neuropsychology The branch of psychology that deals with the relationship between the brain and mental functions.

Non-directional hypothesis Also called a two-tailed or bi-directional hypothesis. It predicts a difference between conditions but not the direction of this difference (cf directional hypothesis).

Non-invasively Examining the brain without actually entering the skull.

Normal distribution curve The symmetrical, bell-shaped curve that represents the distribution of scores on any attribute. Researchers use it to make judgements of how unusual an observation or result is.

Norms Behaviours and values that are the rule or expected in a society/group.

Null hypothesis The hypothesis that predicts no difference on the dependent variable between conditions (see hypothesis; cf experimental hypothesis).

Olfactory To do with the sense of smell.

Open-ended questions Questions which have no predetermined answer.

Order effects Confounding variables arising from the order in which participants experience the conditions of an investigation.

Participant A person who takes part in research.

Peer A person of equal standing with another in terms of, for example, rank or age.

Peer review When a piece of research is reviewed by psychologists who are researching and publishing work in the same area (peers). They assess the quality and originality of the research.

Penile plethysmography A measure of physical sexual arousal in men using an instrument that measures variations in the amount of blood in the penis.

PhD This is an abbreviation for 'Doctor of Philosophy' (this term is used for all subjects, not just philosophy). A postgraduate student becomes a Doctor of Philosophy after successfully completing several years' research, writing it up as a thesis and passing an oral examination (a viva).

Phenotypic A phenotype is an individual's unique set of characteristics which we can observe (cf genotype).

Placebo A placebo is a treatment that is inactive itself, but may alleviate an illness. The placebo effect is thought to be psychological or due to other unrelated factors.

Placenta An organ that develops in the uterus of female mammals during pregnancy. The foetus is attached to it by the umbilical cord. It enables oxygen and nutrients to be absorbed into the foetus' blood and carbon dioxide and waste to be released from it.

Population A particular group or a collection of items.

Probability The extent to which something is likely to happen (in research, we never know if the results arose by chance or not, only the probability that they arose by chance).

Psychometric The theory and practice of measuring and/or quantifying aspects of psychological behaviour.

Psychopathology The study of psychological disorders.

Psychotic The state when a person loses contact with reality; when they cannot distinguish their own thoughts, ideas, perceptions and imaginings from reality.

Reductionist Explaining behaviour by simply reducing it to its basic parts, such as the action of brain cells or chemicals.

Reliable In research, knowing that the findings would be the same each time the research was conducted.

Replication/replicate Repeating an investigation/trial to obtain a consistent result.

Research Systematic investigation and study in order to establish facts and reach new conclusions.

Research methods The techniques used in systematic investigation to gather information (e.g. surveys, observations).

Rorschach ink-blot technique A test, devised by Hermann Rorschach in the 1920s, which is most commonly used in psychoanalysis. In the test a person is shown a standard set of symmetrical ink blots on cards. They describe what they see in the ink blot and the therapist questions them and interprets their response.

Sample A portion of a population from which the attributes of the whole population can be estimated.

Schizoaffective disorder A disorder where a person has the symptoms of schizophrenia but also has episodes of depression and mania.

Significance/significant The extent to which a result deviates from that expected to arise simply by chance (e.g. from random variation or errors in sampling).

Single-blind An investigation where information that may bias the results is concealed from either researcher or participant (cf double-blind).

Social facilitation The effect where the mere presence of other people affects a person's performance in a task (increasing or decreasing performance).

Split personality A term which is incorrectly used for schizophrenia. (See multiple personalities).

Standard deviation A quantity which indicates the extent of deviation for a group as a whole (i.e. how much all of the scores in a data set vary around the average score, the mean).

Statistics The science of collecting and analysing numerical data in large quantities. Statistics are especially used to infer proportions in a whole population from those in a sample.

Stimuli Stimuli is the plural of stimulus. A stimulus is an input (object, event or information) that produces a specific reaction.

Theory A supposition or a system of ideas intended to explain something.

Traits Personal qualities or attributes that influence behaviour across situations.

Transcranial magnetic stimulation (TMS) A technique which uses focused pulses of magnetism to induce electrical activity in small groups of cells in the brain.

T-test A statistical test which assesses whether the difference in means between two conditions is significant.

Validity In research, the degree to which a test measures what it is supposed to measure. There are two types of validity. External validity is the extent to which the data collected from a sample can be generalized to the entire population, and across locations, time and measures. Internal validity is the extent to which we can be sure that the independent variable is causing changes in the dependent variable (rather than confounding variables causing the changes).

Variable A factor that varies.

Within-participants (related or repeated-measures) design When participants experience all conditions (cf between-participants design).

References

Ainsworth, M.D.S., Blehar, M., Waters, E. and Wall, S. (1978) *Patterns of Attachment.* Hillsdale, NJ: Erlbaum.

Andreasen, N.C. (1984) *Scale for the Assessment of Positive Symptoms (SAPS).* Iowa City, IA: University of Iowa.

Andreasen, N.C. (1989) Scale for the Assessment of Negative Symptoms (SANS), *British Journal of Psychiatry*, 155(7): 53–8.

APA (1994) *Diagnostic and Statistical Manual of Mental Disorders*, 4th edn. (DSM-IV). Washington, DC: American Psychiatric Association.

Ardelt, M. (2000) Still stable after all these years? Personality stability theory revisited, *Social Psychology Quarterly*, 63(4): 392–405.

Aronson, E. (1988) *The Social Animal.* New York, NY: Freeman.

Avenanti, A., Bueti, D., Galati, G. and Aglioti, S.M. (2005) Transcranial magnetic stimulation highlights the sensorimotor side of empathy for pain, *Nature Neuroscience*, 8(7): 955–60.

Bartlett, F.C. (1932) *Remembering.* Cambridge: Cambridge University Press.

Bates, J.E., Freeland, C.A.B. and Lounsbury, M.L. (1979) Measurement of infant difficultness, *Child Development*, 50: 794–803.

Baumrind, D. (1964) Some thoughts on ethics of research: after reading Milgram's 'Behavioral study of obedience', *American Psychologist*, 19(6): 421–3.

Binet, A. and Simon, T. (1905) Méthodes nouvelles pour le diagnostic du niveau intellectuel des anormaux, *L'Année Psychologique*, 11: 191–244.

Birchwood, M., Smith, J., Cochrane, R., Wetton, S. and Copestake, S. (1990) The Social Functioning Scale: the development and validation of a new scale of social adjustment for use in family intervention programmes with schizophrenic patients, *British Journal of Psychiatry*, 157: 853–9.

Bird, C. (1927) The influence of the press upon the accuracy of report, *Journal of Abnormal and Social Psychology*, 22: 123–9.

Blass, T. (2004) *The Man Who Shocked the World: The Life and Legacy of Stanley Milgram.* New York, NY: Basic Books.

Bleuler, E. (1911) *Dementia Praecox, or the Group of Schizophrenias.* Trans. J. Zinkin and N.D.C. Lewis (1950) New York, NY: International Universities Press.

Bokhorst, C., Bakermans-Kranenburg, M.J., Fearon, R.M.P., Van Ijzendoorn, M.H., Fonagy, P. and Schuengel, C. (2003) The importance of shared environment in mother-infant attachment security: a behavioural genetic study, *Child Development*, 74: 1769–82.

Bradley, B.P., Mogg, K., White, J., Groom, C. and de Bono, J. (1999) Attentional bias for emotional faces in generalized anxiety disorder, *British Journal of Clinical Psychology*, 38: 267–78.

Bransford, J.D. and McCarrell, N.S. (1974) A sketch of a cognitive approach to comprehension: some thoughts about understanding what it means to comprehend, in D. Palerrno and W. Weimer (eds) *Cognition and the Symbolic Processes*. Washington, DC: V.H. Winston and Co.

British Psychological Society (2006) *Code of Ethics and Conduct*. http://www. bps.org.uk/the-society/ethics-rules-charter-code-of-conduct/code-of-conduct/ code-of-conduct_home.cfm (accessed 14 July 2006).

Broca, P. (1861) Remarques sur le siége de la faculté du langage articulé, suivies d'une observation d'aphémie (perte de la parole), *Bulletins de la Société Anatomique*, 6: 330–57. Reprinted as 'Remarks on the seat of the faculty of articulate language, followed by an observation of aphemia' in G. von Bonin (1960) *Some Papers on the Cerebral Cortex*. Springfield, IL: Charles C Thomas.

Butcher, J.N., Dahlstrom, W.G., Graham, J.R., Tellegan, A. and Kaemmer, B. (1989) *Minnesota Multiphasic Personality Inventory-2*. The University of Minnesota Press, Minnesota, MN: Pearson Assessments.

Cattell, R.B. (1957) *Personality and Motivation Structure and Measurement*. New York, NY: Harcourt, Brace and World.

Cattell, R.B., Eber, H.W. and Tatsuoka, M.M. (1970) *The Handbook for the Sixteen Personality Factor Questionnaire*. Champaign, IL: Institute for Personality and Ability Testing.

Ceci, S.J. and Bruck, M. (1995) *Jeopardy in the Courtroom: A Scientific Analysis of Children's Testimony*. Washington, DC: American Psychological Association.

Chekroun, P. and Brauer, M. (2002) The bystander effect and social control behaviour: the effect of the presence of others on people's reactions to norm violations, *European Journal of Social Psychology*, 32: 853–67.

Christensen, L. (1988) Deception in psychological research: when is its use justified? *Personality and Social Psychology Bulletin*, 14(4): 664–75.

Conley, J.J. (1985) Longitudinal stability of personality traits: a multitrait-multimethod-multioccasion analysis, *Journal of Personality and Social Psychology*, 49: 1266–82.

Costa, P.T. Jr. and McCrae, R.R. (1985) *The NEO Personality Inventory Manual*. Odessa, FL: Psychological Assessment Resources.

Costa, P.T. Jr. and McCrae, R.R. (1986) Personality stability and its implications for clinical psychology, *Clinical Psychology Review*, 6: 407–23.

Costa, P.T. Jr. and McCrae, R.R. (1988) Personality in adulthood: a six-year longitudinal study of self-reports and spouse ratings on the NEO Personality Inventory, *Journal of Personality and Social Psychology*, 54(5): 853–63.

Costa, P.T. Jr. and McCrae, R.R. (1992) *Revised NEO Personality Inventory and*

Five-Factor Inventory Professional Manual. Odessa, FL: Psychological Assessment Resources.

Costa, P.T. Jr., McCrae, R.R., Zonderman, A.B., Barbano, H.E., Lebowitz, B. and Larson, D.M. (1986) Cross-sectional studies of personality in a national sample: stability in neuroticism, extraversion and openness, *Psychology and Aging*, 1: 144–9.

Darley, J.M. and Latané, B. (1968) Bystander intervention in emergencies: diffusion of responsibility, *Journal of Personality and Social Psychology*, 8: 377–83.

Darviri, S.V. and Woods, S.A. (2006) Uncertified absence from work and the Big Five: an examination of absence records and future absence intentions, *Personality and Individual Differences*, 41: 356–69.

Darwin, C. (1872) *The Expression of the Emotions in Man and Animals*. New York, NY: D. Appleton.

Darwin, C. (1877) A biographical sketch of an infant, *Mind*, 2: 285–94.

Data Protection Act (1998) Elizabeth II, reprinted April 2005. London: The Stationery Office Limited.

Dement, W. and Kleitman, N. (1957) The relation of eye movements during sleep to dream activity: an objective method for the study of dreaming, *Journal of Experimental Psychology*, 53: 339–46.

DeWolff, M.S. and Van Ijzendoorn, M.H. (1997) Sensitivity and attachment. A meta-analysis on parental antecedents of infant-attachment, *Child Development*, 68: 571–91.

Dohnt, H.K. and Tiggemann, M. (2005) Peer influences on body dissatisfaction and dieting awareness in young girls, *British Journal of Developmental Psychology*, 23: 103–16.

Dovidio, J.F., Piliavin, J.A., Gaertner, S.L., Schroeder, D.A. and Clark, R.D. (1991) The arousal:cost-reward model and the process of intervention: a review of the evidence, *Review of Personality and Social Psychology*, 12: 86–118.

Fearon, R.M.P. (1999) Shared and non-shared influences on the development and attachment in twins. Unpublished doctoral dissertation, University of London.

Fechner, G.T. (1859) Elements of psychophysics, in R.J. Herrnstein and E.G. Boring (eds) (1965) *A Source Book in the History of Psychology*. Cambridge, MA: Harvard University Press.

Fillmore, C.J. (1971) Types of lexical information, in D.D. Steinberg and L.A. Jakobovits (eds) *Semantics: An Interdisciplinary Reader in Philosophy, Linguistics and Psychology*. Cambridge: Cambridge University Press.

Finn, S.E. (1986) Stability of personality self-ratings over 30 years: evidence for an age/cohort interaction, *Journal of Personality and Social Psychology*, 50: 813–18.

Fischer, P., Greitemeyer, T., Pollozek, F. and Frey, D. (2006) The unresponsive bystander: are bystanders more responsive in dangerous emergencies? *European Journal of Social Psychology*, 36: 267–78.

Fiske, D.W. (1949) Consistency of the factorial structures of personality ratings from different sources, *Journal of Abnormal Social Psychology*, 44: 329–44.

Freeman, B., Powell, J., Ball, D., Hill, L., Craig, I. and Plomin, R. (1997) DNA by mail: an inexpensive and non-invasive method for collecting DNA samples from widely dispersed populations, *Behaviour Genetics*, 27: 251–7.

Fritsch, G. and Hitzig, E. (1870) Über die elektrische Erregbarkeit des Grosshirns. Archiv für Anatomie und Physiologie, 300–32. Translated as 'On the electrical excitability of the cerebrum' in G. von Bonin (ed.) (1960) *Some Papers on the Cerebral Cortex*. Springfield, IL: Charles C Thomas.

Galton, F. (1888) Head growth in students at the University of Cambridge, *Nature*, 38: 14–15.

Garcia, S.M., Weaver, K., Moskowitz, G.B. and Darley, J.M. (2002) Crowded minds: the implicit bystander effect, *Journal of Personality and Social Psychology*, 83(4): 843–53.

Gardner, D.S. (1933) The perception and memory of witnesses, *Cornell Law Quarterly*, 8: 391–409.

Gaudiano, B.A. (2005) Cognitive behaviour therapies for psychotic disorders: current empirical status and future directions, *Clinical Psychology: Science and Practice*, 12: 33–50.

Geiselman, R.E., Fisher, R.P., MacKinnon, D.P. and Holland, H.L. (1985) Eyewitness memory enhancement in the police interview: cognitive retrieval mnemonics versus hypnosis, *Journal of Applied Psychology*, 70: 401–12.

Gignac, G., Vernon, P.A. and Wickett, J.C. (2003) Factors influencing the relationship between brain size and intelligence, in H. Nyborg (ed.) *The Scientific Study of General Intelligence: Tribute to Arthur R. Jensen*. New York, NY: Pergamon.

Glass, G.V. (1976) Primary, secondary, and meta-analysis of research, *The Educational Researcher*, 10: 3–8.

Goldsmith, H.H. (1991) A zygosity questionnaire for young twins: a research note, *Behaviour Genetics*, 21: 257–69.

Gould, R.A., Mueser, K.T., Bolton, E., Mays, E. and Goff, D. (2001) Cognitive therapy for psychosis in schizophrenia: an effect size analysis, *Schizophrenia Research*, 48: 335–42.

Grossmann, K.E. and Grossmann, K. (1991) Attachment quality as an organizer of emotional and behavioural responses in a longitudinal perspective, in C.M. Parkes, J. Stevenson-Hinde and P. Marris (eds) *Attachment Across the Life Cycle*. London/New York: Tavistock/ Routledge.

Gumley, A., O'Grady, M., McNay, L., Reilly, J., Power, K. and Norrie, J. (2003) Early intervention for relapse in schizophrenia: results of a 12-month randomized controlled trial of cognitive-behavioural therapy, *Psychological Medicine*, 33: 419–31.

Haddock, G., Barrowclough, C., Tarrier, N., Moring, J., O'Brien, R., Schofield, N., Quinn, J., Palmer, S., Davies, L., Lowens, I., McGovern, J and Lewis, S.W. (2003) Cognitive-behavioural therapy and motivational intervention for schizophrenia and substance misuse: 18 month outcomes of a randomized controlled trial, *British Journal of Psychiatry*, 183: 418–26.

Hamilton, J.A. (1935) The association between brain size and maze ability in the white rat. Unpublished doctoral dissertation, University of California, Berkeley.

Haney, C., Banks, W.C. and Zimbardo, P.G. (1973) Study of prisoners and guards in a simulated prison, *Naval Research Reviews*, 9: 1–17.

Harari, H., Harari, O. and White, R.V. (1985) The reaction to rape by American male bystanders, *Journal of Social Psychology*, 125: 653–8.

Hathaway, S.R. and McKinley, J.C. (1940) *The Minnesota Multiphasic Personality Inventory (MMPI) Manual*. New York, NY: Psychological Corporation.

Heap, M. (ed.) (1988) *Hypnosis: Current Clinical, Experimental and Forensic Practises*. London: Croom Helm.

Holliday, R.E. and Albon, A.J. (2004) Minimizing misinformation effects in young children with cognitive interview mnemonics, *Applied Cognitive Psychology*, 18: 263–81.

Huff, C.R. (1987) Wrongful conviction: societal tolerance of injustice. *Research in Social Problems and Public Policy*, 4: 99–115.

Hunter, J.E. and Schmidt, F.L. (1990) *Methods of Meta-Analysis: Correcting Error and Bias in Research Findings*. Newbury Park, CA: Sage Publications.

Hunter, J.E. and Schmidt, F.L. (2004) *Methods of Meta-Analysis: Correcting Error and Bias in Research Findings*. Thousand Oaks, CA: Sage Publications.

Ivanovic, D.M., Leiva, B.P., Castro, C.G., Olivares, M.G., Jansana, J.M.M. and Castro, V.G. (2004) Brain development parameters and intelligence in Chilean high school graduates. *Intelligence*, 32: 461–79.

James, W. (1890) *The Principles of Psychology*. New York, NY: Henry Holt.

Kaufman, G. and Elder, G.H. Jr. (2003) Grandparenting and age identity. *Journal of Aging Studies*, 17: 269–82.

Kelemen, W.L. and Creeley, C.E. (2003) State-dependent memory effects using caffeine and placebo do not extend to metamemory, *Journal of General Psychology*, 130(1): 70–86.

Kimmel, A.J. (1998) In defence of deception, *American Psychologist*, 53(7): 803–4.

Kraepelin, E. (1883) *Compendium der Psychiatrie*. Leipzig: Abel.

Lakatos, K., Toth, I., Nemoda, Z., Ney, K., Sasvari-Szekely, M. and Gervai, J. (2000) Dopamine D4 receptor (DRD4) gene polymorphism is associated with attachment disorganization in infants. *Molecular Psychiatry*, 5: 633–7.

Lange, W.G.T., Tierney, K.J., Reinhardt-Rutland, A.H. and Vivekananda-Schmidt, P. (2004) Viewing behaviour of spider phobics and non-phobics in the presence of threat and safety stimuli, *British Journal of Clinical Psychology*, 43: 235–43.

Latané, B. and Darley, J.M. (1968) Group inhibition of bystander intervention, *Journal of Personality and Social Psychology*, 10: 215–21.

Latané, B. and Darley, J.M. (1970) *The Unresponsive Bystander: Why Doesn't he Help?* New York, NY: Appleton-Century-Crofts.

Latané, B. and Nida, S. (1981) Ten years of research on group size and helping, *Psychological Bulletin*, 89: 308–24.

Latané, B. and Rodin, J. (1969) A lady in distress: inhibiting effects of friends and strangers on bystander intervention, *Journal of Experimental Social Psychology*, 5: 189–202.

Le Bon, G. (1896) *The Crowd*. London: Fisher Unwin.

Leon, G.R., Gillum, B., Gillum, R. and Gouze, M. (1979) Personality stability and change over a 30-year period: middle age to old age, *Journal of Consulting and Clinical Psychology*, 47: 517–24.

Leve, L.D., Winebarger, A.A., Fagot, B.I., Reid, J.B. and Goldsmith, H.H. (1998) Environmental and genetic variance in children's observed and reported maladaptive behaviour, *Child Development*, 69: 1286–98.

Loftus, E.F. and Palmer, J.C. (1974) Reconstruction of automobile destruction: an example of the interaction between language and memory, *Journal of Verbal Learning and Verbal Behaviour*, 13: 585–9.

MacLullich, A.M.J., Ferguson, K.L., Deary, I.J., Seckl, J.R., Starr, J.M. and Wardlaw, J.M. (2002) Intercranial capacity and brain volumes are associated with cognition in elderly men, *Neurology*, 59: 169–74.

Main, M. (1999) Attachment theory: eighteen points with suggestions for future studies, in J. Cassidy and P.R. Shaver (eds) *Handbook of Attachment: Theory, Research and Clinical Applications*. New York, NY: Guildford.

Main, M. and Cassidy, J. (1988) Categories of response to reunion with the parent at age six: predictable from infant attachment classifications and stable over a one-month period, *Developmental Psychology*, 24(3): 415–26.

Main, M. and Solomon, J. (1986) Discovery of an insecure-disorganized/disoriented attachment pattern, in T.B. Brazelton and M. Yogman (eds) *Affective Development in Infancy*. Norwood, NJ: Ablex.

Main, M. and Solomon, J. (1990) Procedures for identifying infants as disorganized/disoriented during the Ainsworth strange situation, in M.T. Greenberg, D. Cicchetti and E.M. Cummings (eds) *Attachment in the Preschool Years: Theory, Research and Intervention*. The John D. and Catherine T. MacArthur Foundation series on Mental Health and Development (pp. 121–60). Chicago, IL: University of Chicago Press.

Main, M., Kaplan, N. and Cassidy, J. (1985) Security in infancy, childhood and adulthood: a move to the level of representation, *Monographs of the Society for Research in Child Development*, 50: 66–104.

Marshall, J. (1969) *Law and Psychology in Conflict*. New York, NY: Anchor Books.

McCrae, R.R. (1982) Consensual validation of personality traits: evidence from self-reports and ratings, *Journal of Personality and Social Psychology*, 43: 293–303.

McCrae, R.R. and Costa, P.T. Jr. (1983) Joint factors in self-reports and ratings: neuroticism, extraversion and openness to experience, *Personality and Individual Differences*, 4: 245–55.

McCrae, R.R. and Costa, P.T. Jr. (1984) *Emerging Lives, Enduring Dispositions: Personality in Adulthood.* Boston, MA: Little, Brown.

McCrae, R.R. and Costa, P.T. Jr. (1987). Validation of the five-factor model of personality across instruments and observers, *Journal of Personality and Social Psychology*, 52: 81–90.

McDaniel, M.A. (2005) Big-brained people are smarter: a meta-analysis of the relationship between in vivo brain volume and intelligence, *Intelligence*, 33: 337–46.

McGuffin, P., Riley, B. and Plomin, R. (2001) Toward behavioural genetics, *Science*, 291: 1232–49.

Milgram, S. (1963) Behavioural study of obedience, *Journal of Abnormal and Social Psychology*, 67(4): 371–8.

Milgrom, J., Negri, L.M., Gemmill, A.W., McNeil, M. and Martin, P.R. (2005) A randomized controlled trial of psychological interventions for postnatal depression, *British Journal of Clinical Psychology*, 44: 529–42.

Mogg, K. and Bradley, B.P. (1998) A cognitive-motivational analysis of anxiety, *Behaviour Research and Therapy*, 36: 809–48.

Neale, M.C., Boker, S.M., Xie, G. and Maes, H.H. (1999) *Mx: Statistical Modelling*, 5th edn. Richmond, VA: Virginia Commonwealth University, Department of Psychiatry.

Nguyen, N.T. and McDaniel, M.A. (2000) Brain size and intelligence: a meta-analysis. Paper presented at the First Annual Conference of the International Society of Intelligence Research, Cleveland, OH.

Nijstad, B.A., Stroebe, W. and Lodewijkx, H.F.M. (2006) The illusion of group productivity: a reduction of failures explanation, *European Journal of Social Psychology*, 36: 31–48.

Norman, W.T. (1963) Toward an adequate taxonomy of personality attributes: replicated factor structure in peer nomination personality ratings, *Journal of Abnormal and Social Psychology*, 66: 574–83.

O'Connor, T.G. and Croft, C.M. (2001) A twin study of attachment in preschool children, *Child Development*, 72: 1501–11.

O'Connor, T.G., Croft, C.M. and Steele, H. (2000) The contributions of behavioural genetic studies to attachment theory, *Attachment and Human Development*, 2: 107–22.

Öhman, A., Flykt, A. and Lundqvist, D. (1999) Unconscious emotion: evolutionary perspectives, psychophysical data and neuropsychological mechanisms, in R.L.A.L. Nadel (ed.) *The Cognitive Neuroscience of Emotion*. New York, NY: Oxford University Press.

Pennington, B.F., Filipek, P.A., Lefly, D., Chhabildas, N., Kennedy, D.N. and Simon, J.H. (2000) A twin MRI study of size variations in the human brain, *Journal of Cognitive Neuroscience*, 12(1): 223–32.

Piliavin, I.M., Rodin, J. and Piliavin, J.A. (1969) Good Samaritanism: an underground phenomenon? *Journal of Personality and Social Psychology*, 13: 289–99.

Pilling, S., Bebbington, P., Kuipers, E., Garety, P., Geddes, J., Martindale, B., Orbach, G. and Morgan, C. (2002) Psychological treatments in schizophrenia: meta-analysis of family intervention and cognitive behaviour therapy, *Psychological Medicine*, 32: 763–82.

QAA (2000) *The Quality Assurance Agency for Higher Education Subject Overview Report Psychology 1998 to 2000*. http://www.qaa.ac.uk/reviews/default.asp (accessed 24 January 2006).

Ricciuti, A.E. (1992) Child-mother attachment: a twin study, *Dissertation Abstracts International*, 54: 364.

Rothbart, M.K. (1981) Measurement of temperament in infancy, *Child Development*, 52: 569–78.

Rushton, J.P. and Ankney, C.D. (1996) Brain size and cognitive ability: correlations with age, sex, social class and race. *Psychonomic Bulletin and Review*, 3: 21–36.

Schwartz, S.H. and Clausen, G.T. (1970) Responsibility, norms, and helping in an emergency, *Journal of Personality and Social Psychology*, 16: 299–310.

Schwartz, S.H. and Gottlieb, A. (1976) Bystander reactions to a violent theft: crime in Jerusalem, *Journal of Personality and Social Psychology*, 34: 1188–99.

Shinn, M.W. (1900) *The Biography of a Baby*. Boston, MA: Houghton Mifflin.

Spangler, G., Fremmer-Bombik, E. and Grossmann, K. (1996) Social and individual determinants of infant attachment security and disorganization, *Infant Mental Health Journal*, 17: 127–39.

Spencer, H. (1855) *The Principles of Psychology*. London: Williams and Norgate.

Sperry, R. (1968) Hemisphere deconnection and unity in conscious awareness, *American Psychologist*, 23(10): 723–33.

Staff, R.T. (2002) Personal communication to Michael A. McDaniel cited in M.A. McDaniel (2005) Big-brained people are smarter: a meta-analysis of the relationship between in vivo brain volume and intelligence, *Intelligence*, 33: 337–46.

Startup, M., Jackson, M.C. and Bendix, S. (2004) North Wales randomized controlled trial of cognitive behaviour therapy for acute schizophrenia spectrum disorders: outcomes at 6 and 12 months, *Psychological Medicine*, 34: 413–22.

Startup, M., Jackson, M.C., Evans, K.E. and Bendix, S. (2005) North Wales randomized controlled trial of cognitive behaviour therapy for acute schizophrenia spectrum disorders: two-year follow-up and economic evaluation, *Psychological Medicine*, 35: 1307–16.

Szasz, T. S. (1960) The myth of mental illness, *American Psychologist*, 15: 113–18.

Tarrier, N., Kinney, C., McCarthy, E., Humphreys, L., Wittowski, A. and Morris, J. (2000) Two-year follow-up of cognitive-behavioral therapy and supportive counselling in the treatment of persistent symptoms in chronic schizophrenia, *Journal of Consulting and Clinical Psychology*, 68: 917–22.

Tarrier, N., Lewis, S., Haddock, G., Bentall, R., Drake, R., Kinderman, P., Kingdon, D., Siddle, R., Everitt, J., Leadley, K., Benn, A., Grazebrook, K., Haley, C.,

Akhtar, S., Davies, L., Palmer, S. and Dunn, G. (2004) Cognitive-behavioural therapy in first-episode and early schizophrenia: 18 month follow-up of a randomized controlled trial, *British Journal of Psychiatry*, 104: 231–9.

Thompson, P.M., Cannon, T.D., Narr, K.L., Erp, T.V., Poutanen, V.P. and Huttunen, M. (2001) Genetic influences on brain structure, *Nature Neuroscience*, 4(12): 1253–8.

Tiedmann, F. (1836) Sur l'encéphale du Nègree compare à celui de l'Europèen et celui de l'orangoutang. Philosophical Transactions of London, cited in J.A. Hamilton (1935) The association between brain size and maze ability in the white rat. Unpublished doctoral dissertation. University of California, Berkeley.

Tipples, J., Young, A.W., Quinlan, P., Broks, P. and Ellis, A.W. (2002) Searching for threat, *The Quarterly Journal of Experimental Psychology*, 55A(3): 1007–26.

Tramo, M.J., Loftus, W.C., Stukel, T.A., Green, R.L., Weaver, J.B. and Gazzaniga, M.S. (1998) Brain size, head size and intelligence quotient in monozygotic twins, *Neurology*, 50(5): 1246–52.

Triplett, N. (1898) The dynamogenic factors in pacemaking and competition, *American Journal of Psychology*, 9: 507–33.

Van Coillie, H., Van Mechelen, I. and Ceulemans, E. (2006) Multidimensional individual differences in age-related behaviours, *Personality and Individual Differences*, 41: 27–38.

Van Ijzendoorn, M.H. (1995) Of the way we are: on temperament, attachment and the transmission gap: A rejoinder to Fox. *Psychological Bulletin*, 117(3): 411–5.

Van Ijzendoorn, M.H. and Kroonenberg, P.M. (1988) Cross-cultural patterns of attachment: a meta-analysis of the strange situation, *Child Development*, 59: 147–56.

Van Ijzendoorn, M.H., Schuengel, C. and Bakermans-Kranenburg, M.J. (1999) Disorganized attachment in early childhood: meta-analysis of precursors, concomitants and sequelae, *Development and Psychopathology*, 11: 225–49.

Van Ijzendoorn, M.H., Moran, G., Belsky, J., Pederson, D., Bakermans-Kranenberg, M.J. and Kneppers, K. (2000) The similarity of siblings' attachments to their mothers, *Child Development*, 71: 1086–98.

Vernon, P.A., Wickett, J.C., Bazana, P.G. and Stelmack, R.M. (2000) The neuropsychology and psychophysiology of human intelligence, in R.J. Sternberg (ed.) *Handbook of Intelligence*. New York, NY: Cambridge University Press.

Walster, E. (1965) The effects of self-esteem on romantic liking, *Journal of Experimental Social Psychology*, 1(2): 184–97.

Watts, F.N. and Sharrock, R. (1984) Questionnaire dimensions of spider phobia, *Behaviour Research and Therapy*, 22: 575–80.

Weiskrantz, L. (1986) *Blindsight: A Case Study and Implications*. Oxford Psychology Series, 12. Oxford: Oxford University Press.

Whalen, P.J., Rauch, S.L., Etcoff, N.L., McInerney, S.C., Lee, M.B. and Jenike, M.A.

(1998) Masked presentations of emotional facial expressions modulate amygdala activity without explicit knowledge, *The Journal of Neuroscience*, 18(1): 411–8.

Whipple, G.M. (1909) The observer as reporter: a survey of the psychology of testimony, *Psychological Bulletin*, 6: 153–70.

Wise, R.A. and Safer, M.A. (2004) What US Judges know and believe about eyewitness testimony, *Applied Cognitive Psychology*, 18: 427–43.

Zimbardo, P.G. (2004) Does psychology make a significant difference in our lives? *American Psychologist*, 59(5): 339–51.

Index